T0112251

A Thyme and Place

Medieval Feasts and Recipes
for the Modern Table

Tricia Cohen and Lisa Graves
Illustrated by Lisa Graves

Skyhorse Publishing

Copyright © 2016 Tricia Cohen and Lisa Graves

All rights to any and all materials in copyright owned by the publisher are strictly reserved by the publisher. All rights reserved. No part of this book may be reproduced in any manner without the express written consent of the publisher, except in the case of brief excerpts in critical reviews or articles. All inquiries should be addressed to Skyhorse Publishing, 307 West 36th Street, 11th Floor, New York, NY 10018.

Skyhorse Publishing books may be purchased in bulk at special discounts for sales promotion, corporate gifts, fund-raising, or educational purposes. Special editions can also be created to specifications. For details, contact the Special Sales Department, Skyhorse Publishing, 307 West 36th Street, 11th Floor, New York, NY 10018 or info@skyhorsepublishing.com.

Skyhorse® and Skyhorse Publishing® are registered trademarks of Skyhorse Publishing, Inc.®, a Delaware corporation.

Visit our website at www.skyhorsepublishing.com.

10 9 8 7 6 5 4 3 2

Library of Congress Cataloging-in-Publication Data is available on file.

Cover design by Jane Sheppard
Cover photo illustration by Lisa Graves

Print ISBN: 978-1-5107-0253-0
Ebook ISBN: 978-1-5107-0254-7

Printed in China

In memory of our fathers, Donald Graves and Walter Sandland, who both passed away during the making of this book.

"I believe that what we become depends on what our fathers teach us at odd moments, when they aren't trying to teach us. We are formed by little scraps of wisdom."

—*Umberto Eco,* Foucault's Pendulum

Special thanks to all of our friends and family who were generous with their input, advice, time, and support including: Michael Cohen, Brian Levey, Kathy Sandland, Sheila Graves, Michael King, Raymond Bewsher, Robert Craig, Edward Branley, the Farrells, Bill Hauris, Irma Thornton, Justin and Sharon Coffini, Kate Devito, Cindy Ennes, and Nelly DaRosso.

Table of Contents

Introduction

Eat, Drink, and Be Medieval

The medieval period, which is split into the Early Middle Ages, the High Middle Ages, and the Late Middle Ages, is loosely defined with regard to exactly where it begins and ends. The term "medieval" was brought about in the nineteenth century to distinguish when history came out of the dark times and entered into what was considered to be the beginning of the modern world. According to many historians, this period began when Rome fell at the end of the fifth century and continued until the sixteenth century (some say fifteenth, others say early seventeenth).

For this book, we have focused primarily on the High Middle Ages and Late Middle Ages up until the mid 1600s (our use of Drambuie in certain recipes, a sweet liqueur, tips us into the eighteenth century . . . but let's just keep moving along). In doing our research, we came across so many interesting holidays, feasts, and celebrations of this period (some hilarious, some quite solemn) that we decided to make it our focus. We've organized the history and recipes of the High Middle Ages by the calendar year—feasting begins with Twelfth Night and ends with Christmas.

There are so many great reasons to cook and, more importantly, to eat! To help you understand why we chose certain ingredients, we've included a brief history behind each holiday. Think how smart you'll sound at your next dinner party when you are able to rattle off strange facts about the history of the Cooper's Hill Cheese Roll or the reason why you made Blackberry Jam on September 29 as opposed to September 30.

No Swans Were Hurt During the Making of This Book

Most of the food consumed during the Middle Ages involved processes and ingredients that are either not readily available—or are simply not palatable today. All of the recipes in this book are based on original recipes from medieval cookbooks and manuscripts that have been adapted and modernized for our contemporary taste buds. What this means is that you won't have to go wandering through the woods with a sword, looking for rare birds and dangerous (and sometimes poisonous) herbs.

One must keep in mind that almost all of the feasts mentioned revolve around the church. Everything was dictated by "holy men"; holidays, food, clothing, customs . . . everything. So, whenever the revelry got out of hand (meaning, they were fun) the religious leaders would often reconstruct celebration guidelines (meaning, they were no longer fun). Along with various well-known figures such as Henry VIII and Oliver Cromwell, clergymen were almost always responsible for these holidays falling out of favor. No one wants to go to a party that forbids fun, or worse . . . booze.

The Medieval Daily Diet

The medieval diet consisted of meat, meat, and more meat. Okay, and some bread. Most of Europe was on a two-meal per day schedule with the first being a dinner at midday and a light supper in the evening.

Farmers and the working folk would have leftovers in the morning for practical reasons. Food preparation took hours (no microwaves), so the earliest a real meal could be served was late afternoon. Thanks to the church, it was considered gluttonous to eat in the morning, but exceptions were made for laborers and children. How kind. Boy, they really had no idea what they were missing. We *love* our breakfast!

As you could probably guess, ingredients we take for granted today were viewed much differently back then. For example, tomatoes were considered poisonous, butter was used to cure flatulence and colicky babies, and any vegetables growing in dirt were thought of as "peasant food."

Food Preparation

Kitchen stoves were not commonplace until the eighteenth century, so most food was prepared directly in a fire. Ovens were used, but mostly in noble households. However, some villages had a "shared" oven for baking bread.

For the most part, food was thrown in a stew pot and placed over a fire. Common cooking methods included roasting, baking, boiling, smoking, and salting. Kitchens were not really built as a separate room until the Late Middle Ages. A giant hearth was most often located in the common living area; as for the nobles, this hearth would be combined with their dining hall.

Many of the tools used are what we use today such as: pots, kettles, skillets, frying pans, etc. There was almost always a large hook that made it easy to swing pots away from the fire to prevent burning and spits for turning roasts so that cooking would be even. Also prevalent was the mortar and sieve. Physicians believed that food should be ground at a very fine consistency to allow for proper digestion, so cooks would mash, sift, and mince ingredients into pastes. Mmmm . . . meat paste.

Most of us today thoroughly enjoy anything to do with baked goods, but in the Middle Ages bread was often considered a cooking vessel. Fruits, meats, and spices were combined and inserted into a molded pastry dish and baked. Stale bread was cut and used as plates called "trenchers," though, depending on your social status, you might also just eat directly off the table.

Mind Your Manners

Despite what you may have heard, people did not eat off the floor, gnaw on giant turkey legs, or wipe their mouths on their shirtsleeves.

It was customary for nobles to clean their hands using a basin of water with linen towels. They did this before every meal. How civilized. Napkins were placed over one's left shoulder or left wrist; elbows were kept off the table; spitting and burping were forbidden; one had to wipe their mouth before sipping from a communal cup, spoons were for broth (so one did not lift a plate up to their mouth; bread was cut, not broken; and, last but not least, prayers were said before *every* meal.

Feeling Tipsy?

One of the common ingredients you'll find in several of these recipes is Drambuie. This delicious liqueur dates back to the eighteenth century (slightly later than the main period focus of this book), and it has a fascinating history. After his defeat at Culloden (April 16, 1746), the Bonnie Prince Charlie (Charles Edward Stuart) went on the run. Charlie managed to escape the mainland by boat, dressed as a woman, and headed for the Isle of Skye. He took refuge with various Highland clans for protection. One of these clan leaders, John MacKinnon, was exceptionally helpful, so much so that the prince rewarded John by giving him a top secret recipe for his own liqueur. Years later, this became what we now call Drambuie.

Drambuie basics: it is a blend of Scotch whisky, herbs, spices, and honey. While it was originally created for medicinal reasons, it is now a popular spirit to be served up straight, mixed in various cocktails, or, in our case, to cook with!

Whisky has much deeper roots in history, with some appearances as far back as the first century, but it grew more mainstream in the fifteenth century as the process of distillation became a fine art. During the Middle Ages, the beverages of choice would be ale, beer, mead, and wine. Along with the Drambuie, you'll find that we've used quite a bit of mead in our recipes, too. Mead is neither wine nor beer. Also called "honey-wine," it is fermented with honey, which gives it a very unique flavor. It is thought to be the oldest fermented beverage in history and could be found in ancient Europe, Africa, and Asia. In fact, the term "honeymoon" traces back to the medieval period and the tradition of the bride and groom drinking mead for a full moon cycle after the marriage—they believed it to be an aphrodisiac. The bride's father would almost always include mead in the dowry, in the hopes that the newlyweds would produce offspring shortly after (or . . . er . . . nine months after) the "I do's."

Spices Were Not Used to Cover the Smell of Rotting Meat!

Many believe that medieval-era food was bland, rotten, and gray. This couldn't be further from the truth. Almost everything was fresh and well seasoned with various spices or sweetened with honey. If you fed your guests meals using more exotic spices, it was a sign of wealth and an indicator of an elevated social status. Keep in mind that, at the time, the spice trade was opening up a world of culinary opportunities (more so for the wealthy, of course). Common and readily available spices included salt, pepper, ginger, cinnamon, cumin, nutmeg, and cloves. Common herbs included sage, parsley, mint, and fennel; however, herbs were primarily used for medicinal purposes.

Common Medieval Herbs and Spices

Nutmeg

Cinnamon

Savory

Marjoram

Ginger

Black Pepper

Cloves

Saffron

Rosemary

White Pepper

Fennel

Parsley

Sage

Cardamom

Hyssop

Anise

Bay Leaves

Basic Recipes

Pump Up the Jam, with Bacon!

We used this on a savory pancake (page 48), but it can also be put out on a charcuterie with cheeses and meats along with your morning eggs, or just take a spoon to the jar.

Ingredients

1½ lbs thick cut bacon cut into 1-inch pieces (we like applewood but any good quality bacon will do)
2 large sweet onions, chopped
4 cloves garlic, minced
6 Mission figs, chopped (optional)
½ cup dark brown sugar, packed
½ cup apple cider vinegar
¼ cup honey
1 Tbsp ground ginger
1 tsp black pepper
6 Tbsp Drambuie (or bourbon—though we liked the sweet notes of Drambuie)
⅛ tsp salt

Directions

⚜ Heat a Dutch oven over medium heat and add the bacon. Cover and cook for approximately 25 minutes. Check on the bacon with some frequency, giving it a stir each time.

⚜ Once the bacon begins to crisp, remove the cover and cook for another 5 minutes. Turn the heat off once the bacon is fully crisp. Remove bacon using a slotted spoon and set aside on a paper towel–lined plate. Let the fat in the Dutch oven cool for a few minutes and then—hear us out—save the stuff in a container for future cooking.

⚜ Leave all but 2 tablespoons of bacon fat in the Dutch oven. Turn the heat back on (again, medium) and add the onions and garlic, scraping up any delicious bacon bits from the bottom of the pan, and cook until soft. Once it is soft, add the figs if you so choose (highly recommended).

⚜ Drop the heat to medium low and add the brown sugar, cider vinegar, honey, ginger, pepper, and Drambuie. Cook for 10 minutes, just enough time for the mixture to start to get jammy.

⚜ Adjust the heat to medium for 5 minutes. Stir frequently to prevent the jam from sticking to the bottom of the pan. Lower heat back down to medium low and add the bacon. Cook for 20 minutes, covered. Stir occasionally. Remove lid and cook for 5 more minutes. Add the salt.

⚜ Remove from heat and let it cool slightly. Add the mixture to the food processor and chop to desired texture. We like it finely chopped as it looks more refined. Well, as refined as bacon jam can be.

Perfect Pasta

This recipe comes from Gloria Fortunato at the Wild Rosemary Bistro in Pittsburgh. Gloria is not only a fantastic chef but also a dear friend. While we were making pasta, Gloria made it clear to us that we should never be worried that the pasta dough would not come out right—you can always adjust as you go. Be confident, and it will turn out the way you want it to. Thanks, Gloria!

Ingredients

3 cups pasta flour or "OO" flour
1 tsp salt
4 large eggs
2 Tbsp extra virgin olive oil
Warm water

Directions

❧ Using a food processor with the metal blade, add the flour into the container along with the salt. Cover and turn the machine on, adding one egg at a time followed by the olive oil. We find it helpful to crack the eggs before starting the process so that you can capture any loose shells.

❧ If the dough does not appear to be coming together, make adjustments. If too dry, add some warm water. It too wet, add a sprinkle of flour. At this point, you can also add some fresh herbs like flat-leaf parsley.

❧ Once the dough comes together into a ball-like shape, turn the machine off and remove the dough onto a floured surface. Make a nice round ball, cut into 3 pieces, wrap in plastic wrap (tightly, don't let any air get to your masterpiece), and place in the refrigerator.

❧ Once chilled, use a pasta machine or, if you are ambitious, hand roll to the desired pasta shape. If using a machine, you may have to run the dough through several times to achieve the right consistency.

Sandland Savory Piecrust

This recipe comes from Tricia's mother, Kathy. She has used this recipe for decades. This is not a delicate crust and is perfect for heavier recipes. Foolproof and easy to create—our favorite! This recipe will yield four rounds of dough. If you are making a pie with a lid, you will only be using two rounds of dough.

Ingredients

1 lb lard
1 tsp salt
1 cup *boiling* water
2 tsp baking powder
6 cups all-purpose flour

Directions

- Place lard in a large bowl, slightly softened. Add the salt to the top of the lard, followed by the boiling water. Mix until the lard is broken up.

- Next, add the dry ingredients over the lard and, using your hands, gently incorporate all the ingredients until it forms the dough. Break the dough into 4 pieces, firmly wrap with plastic wrap, and place into refrigerator until cooled, but not cold.

- If you are making this in advance and the dough is cold, remove from the refrigerator until it starts to soften. Roll out dough on a floured surface.

Parsley Oil

This is a great way to use fresh herbs or even to preserve your herbs at the end of the summer. You can use this cooking process with any herb, but you may want to consider using different oils or a combination of oils (for example, walnut and olive oil).

Ingredients

2 cups fresh flat-leaf parsley, stems off *(as best as you can before you go crazy)*
1 cup olive oil
Salt

Directions

❧ Bring about 2 cups of salted water to a boil. Add the fresh parsley for 15–20 seconds. Using a slotted spoon, immediately remove the blanched herbs and place them in a bowl of ice water. This will stop the cooking process. Once the parsley has cooled completely, remove the herb from the water and wring out the water using paper towels.

❧ Add the parsley and oil to a food processor for about 30 seconds or so. Drain the oil through a fine sieve and now you have beautifully colored and flavored oil.

❧ Store the oil in a refrigerator for 2 weeks. We chose to pour it into a silicone ice tray; ours was in the shape of hearts. Freeze the oil and then pop them out of the tray into a freezer bag. If they are not coming out easily from the tray, just heat slightly with hot water at the bottom of the mold. This is a perfect way to add oil to salads, pasta, or really anything else.

Girdle Crackers

Using stones to cook bread goes back to the beginning of time. The Scottish made bread cooked on a bannock stone. This treasured family stone was passed down from generation to generation. The English and Irish used a piece of sandstone, called a girdle, to make bread from the fifth to fifteenth century. The "bread" was a staple food for many who hailed from the British Empire. We used a pan—but please don't call it pan bread.

Ingredients

2 cups all-purpose flour
1 tsp salt
3 Tbsp lard, plus extra for the pan (we do not recommend using vegetable shortening)
2 Tbsp mead (or another sweet white wine)
2 large eggs
Herbs (to season; optional)

Directions

⚜ Step one, and most important: remove any rings from your fingers. You will thank us later. In a large bowl, sift the flour and salt. Using your hands, mix the lard into the flour and salt until the combination resembles sand.

⚜ Beat the mead and eggs together in a separate bowl. Pour the liquid into the dry ingredients. Add a bit extra mead or cold water if the mixture is dry. This is the time you can add your herbs, if you so choose. We recommend finely cutting up a mixture of sage, thyme, and rosemary.

⚜ Mix the ingredients well and then roll out the dough on a floured surface until thin. Using a cutter (a biscuit cutter works wonderfully), cut the dough into circles. Heat a large, heavy frying pan with lard. Add the dough rounds to the pan, working in batches. If the pan is warm enough, you will only need to turn them once. This happens quickly, especially if the rounds are thin, so stay alert.

⚜ Remove from pan and add a generous amount of sea salt or serve plain. This is best served warm and bite-sized.

Ideas for Serving

Compound herb or sea salt butter
Bacon jam (page 16)
Shrimp & Lobster in Vinegar
(page 83)

Medieval Holidays & Feasts

Celebrate medieval holidays throughout the year! Each feast includes information on the original food served in medieval times, why and when the feast was observed, and a modern-day recipe using readily available ingredients that recognize and celebrate the essence of the original feast (and, don't worry, we did not cook a hog's head or a peacock!).

Twelfth Night

January 5th or 6th
Celebration of the coming of Epiphany. The last holiday before everyone went back to work. Hoorah!

The History
New Year, New Pudding
This festival celebrates the coming of Epiphany (the celebration of God the Son as a human being, Jesus Christ). It also concludes the twelve days of Christmas.

In medieval times, Twelfth Night meant the end of an entire festival season that began with All Hallows' Eve in October. It was the final day of indulging in holiday food and drink before the villagers had to go back to work (and back to their diets of less-than-indulgent food).

King of the Bean, Queen of the Pea
One of the many traditions observed on this night was to eat a cake with a bean and a pea hidden inside (ahem . . . choking hazard). Those who found the bean and pea would be declared the king and queen of the feast, and their "reign" would end at midnight.

In France, the Twelfth Night cake was called *tortell*, an O-shaped pastry stuffed with marzipan and topped with glazed fruit. In Spain, this cake was called *roscón de reyes*.

Revelers often drank wassail on Christmas and Twelfth Night. Wassail is similar to mulled cider, but is more or less a mulled beer. Drinking

Troubadours were traveling musicians who composed and performed songs at most medieval celebrations. They were lyrical poets who sang of battles, love, and chivalry to the lords, nobles, and royalty.

large quantities ensured a good apple harvest for the coming year (and quite possibly a ferocious hangover).

Cromwell: Pudding and Party Killer
Also a popular dish on this day was fig or plum pudding. This dish dates back to the mid 1600s. It was banned, along with Yule logs, caroling, and nativity scenes by none other than Oliver Cromwell (grrrr) who thought all the celebrations were too pagan. Oh, Oliver.

Good Queen's Wassail

Mulled cider for a noble New Year. You will need a cheesecloth.

Ingredients

1 bottle Riesling or another mildly sweet
  white wine
2 cups honey
1 Tbsp each ground ginger, cinnamon,
  cardamom, white pepper, clove, nutmeg, and
  caraway seeds
2 tsp white pepper
Apple cider

Directions

⚜ Bring the wine and honey to a boil. Skim the scum (bubbles) off of the top as it boils. This very necessary process is to clarify the honey.

⚜ Remove from heat, stir in the spices, and store covered in the refrigerator for 12–24 hours.

⚜ Strain the mixture through cheesecloth but don't try to capture the entire residue, as you want the residual spices to blend with the wine mixture for the next month in the refrigerator. Once it is set for one month (or longer), take the mixture out of the refrigerator and let it sit for an hour. The honey and spices will be at the bottom in a solid mass. Warming it up a bit will allow you to mix all those great flavors together in a few good shakes.

⚜ Strain the mixture, twice, through cheesecloth, and set aside. Warm a container of apple cider on the stove top. Take out a small punch bowl and add the wassail mix. Fill with warm apple cider and stir. We also suggest adding some bourbon to really get your Twelfth Night party going. Garnish with orange slices and cinnamon sticks.

Start this one month before the party! Store in the fridge and take out an hour before guests arrive. Easy-peasy cider cocktail at the ready! Feel free to add a touch (or more) of bourbon.

Twelfth Night: Or King and Queen

by Robert Herrick (1591–1674)

Now, now the mirth comes
With the cake full of plums,
Where bean's the king of the sport here;
Beside we must know,
The pea also
Must revel, as queen, in the court here.

Begin then to choose,
This night as ye use,
Who shall for the present delight here,
Be a king by the lot,
And who shall not
Be Twelfth-day queen for the night here.

Which known, let us make
Joy-sops with the cake;
And let not a man then be seen here,
Who unurg'd will not drink
To the base from the brink
A health to the king and queen here.

Next crown a bowl full
With gentle lamb's wool:
Add sugar, nutmeg, and ginger,
With store of ale too;
And thus ye must do
To make the wassail a swinger.

Give then to the king
And queen wassailing:
And though with ale ye be whet here,
Yet part from hence
As free from offence
As when ye innocent met here.

Plough Monday

Monday after January 6th

Celebrated all day. Get your pudding on, don't get punked, and give them a penny already.

The History

Back to Work!

Plough Monday was celebrated throughout the United Kingdom on the Monday after January 6th, or the first Monday after the Twelfth Night of Epiphany. This day marked the return to agricultural work

after Christmas. During the holidays, work was scarce, so this feast was held in hope that jobs and harvests would be plentiful in the coming months.

Plough Pranks

Farmers would take their ploughs to the church to be blessed the day before (Plough Sunday). On the following day, they walked through the villages with decorated ploughs to raise money and chanted "Penny for the plough boys!" This was a happy day; there was singing, dancing, musicians, a person dressed as the "Bessy," and another as the "Fool."

Costumes were to add to the merriment, but they also doubled as a disguise so that there was no embarrassment when visiting the homes of residents (usually the homes of the wealthier landowners) who did not wish to contribute. Those who did not throw money in the plough were often the victims of a prank or two later that night (plough tracks across their lawn). One could guess that the pranks were on par with how much drinking was involved.

References to Plough Monday date back to the late thirteenth century when "plough candles" were lit in various churches, but most of the observances declined in the nineteenth century.

Back to the food: a very specific meal was always served on Plough Monday—plough pudding. This savory meat pie consisted of rendered suet, pork sausage, bacon, sage, and onions encased in a pastry crust. While most of the ingredients are readily available in today's markets, our modern-day palates require some refining. The word "pudding" comes from the French word *boudin*, which means "small sausage" (insert inappropriate jokes here). During medieval times, "pudding" was a term used for meats and other ingredients that were encased in a pastry or dough and then baked, steamed, or boiled.

Don't worry, we have not developed anything with rendered suet. We've used breakfast sausage, apples, and sage for our pudding to give it a bit more depth. Making a traditional English pudding requires different techniques and a change of mindset for those of us living in the United States, where "pudding" is strictly a dessert!

Plough Pudding

Enough to share, but you may not want to.

Ingredients

2 cups all-purpose flour
1 Tbsp baking powder
1 tsp sea salt
6 Tbsp vegetable shortening (plus extra for greasing the basin)
½ cup quartered apples
1 lb sweet pork sausage, bulk (not in the casing)
½ tsp black pepper
1 Tbsp fresh sage, finely chopped
3 slices thickly cut bacon, chopped (we used applewood for that extra flavor)
3 breakfast sausage links, quartered
1 large shallot, finely chopped
2 Tbsp brown sugar, tightly packed
Cold water

- The first thing to note is that you do need to buy a pudding pot, otherwise known as a pudding basin. This is not a container you can pluck from your cabinet; it needs to be one that can handle the type of cooking that a pudding requires. Amazon is always a great source for these "hard to find" cooking items. We purchased a .95-quart and it worked perfectly.
- Makes six generous servings or *one* giant serving, depending on how hungry you are or if you feel like sharing after all that hard work! We won't judge.
- This is a savory *meat* pudding! Don't invite any vegetarians.

Directions

⚜ Generously grease the pudding basin with extra shortening and set aside.

For the crust:

⚜ Measure the flour, baking powder, and salt into a bowl, and stir to combine. Add the shortening and rub together until mixture resembles coarse sand. Use your hands! Slowly, start to add water until the dough comes together. We used half a cup of water.

⚜ Using your dough-covered hands, plop the dough onto a flour-covered surface. Knead in the flour and make a dough ball. Cut into three equal parts. Wrap each separately in plastic wrap and tuck into the refrigerator. Make sure the plastic wrap tightly covers all parts of the dough to prevent air from getting in. This is a savory dough, which means it will be heavy and will look "imperfect."

⚜ Remove two of the sections from the refrigerator after it has been chilled, a half hour or so, enough time for you to clean your hands and the mess you just made. Combine the two sections and roll out on a lightly floured surface until ⅛-inch thick and somewhat round, but again this does not need to be perfect; it just has to be big enough to line the basin. Hold the flattened dough in your hands and carefully hold it over the basin. Drop the center of the dough in first and follow with the sides to get out any air bubbles, until your basin is properly lined. Press the dough down in the center followed by the sides. Trim any dough that is not even with the top of the basin. Use the trimmed dough to fill in any tears or gaps.

For the filling:

- Parboil the quartered apple. We left the skin on for texture and color. Once done, remove the apple quarters from the hot water and let cool. Then, you can cut them up nicely into bite-size pieces.

- In a bowl, combine the bulk sausage, pepper, and sage. Once it is fully combined, press the mixture evenly into the dough in the center and sides. In a separate bowl, combine the bacon, breakfast sausage, shallot, apple, and brown sugar. Add this mixture to the center of the pudding basin. Press down on it a bit to make sure it is even with the top.

- Finally, roll out the remaining chilled third piece of dough like you did with the other pieces. Brush some water onto the dough in the pudding basin so you can get a nice seal. Place the remaining dough onto the top of the basin and press firmly on the edges to seal. Again, trim off extra dough.

- This is the part you want to take your time with. Cover the top with parchment paper. This should overlap, followed by a piece of aluminum foil (we prefer heavy grade). Wrap kitchen twine around the edge of the basin, locking the foil and paper into place. We trim any excess materials so the water doesn't get into the basin.

- Put the basin into a large pot. The pot should be large enough for you to be able to maneuver it when there is hot water boiling! Pour water into the pot, around the basin, until the water is reaches ¾ of the way up the basin. Try to avoid getting water on top of the basin. Boil the water for 4 hours—yes, 4 hours. As the water starts to evaporate, fill it up with hot water from the kettle. This is a long process that requires your attention, but it will be worth it.

- Carefully remove the basin from the pot and let cool. Remove the paper and foil, and discard. Use a sharp paring knife, to go around the sides ever so gently; don't puncture the golden crust. This will not take much effort; it just needs a little nudge. We placed a plate on the top of the basin and then flipped it over. The basin should come off easily. Dig in.

St. Brigid's Day and Candlemas

February 1st and 2nd
Get the plough out and maybe write a poem about sheep.

The History

Candlemas is the Christian festival commemorating the Purification of the Blessed Virgin and the Presentation of Jesus in the Temple. The name "Candlemas" is derived from the procession of candles, inspired by the words found in the Bible "a light to lighten the Gentiles."

This date is significant because it falls right in the middle of the winter solstice and the spring equinox. All celebrations surrounding these two seasonal events involved farming and ploughing the fields. The cattle and sheep would be brought out of the winter pastures so that crops could be planted.

Get in My Belly!
The day before Candlemas, February 1, is known as St. Brigid's Day, and it marks the beginning of spring. St. Brigid, the patron saint of poetry and wisdom, was associated with all regeneration and nature's bounty. The eternal flame for Brigid was lit in her honor at the St. Brigid's Cathedral in Kildare. In the thirteenth century,

SAVE YOURSELVES! Celebrate Candlemas with a St. Brigid's cross. These crosses were woven on the day of the feast and set over doorways and windows as a symbol of protection.

nuns took over the flame, forbidding any men to enter the premises until an angry bishop came along and had it extinguished for the first time in a thousand years. We're guessing that he wasn't invited to the feast. In Ireland, this day is also referred to as Imbolc, which translates to "in the belly," a reference to pregnant, lactating sheep, that were symbols of the first hints of spring.

Because Candlemas and St. Brigid's Feast or Imbolc are celebrations of the milk that began to flow forth from the sheep in the wake of spring, dairy is the star ingredient. Cheeses, milk, butter, cream, and yogurt could all be incorporated into your meal, be it breakfast, lunch, or dinner.

Bread Winner
Braided bread is found in many forms and in many cultures. They are readily available at almost any supermarket or bakery and are the perfect accompaniment for whatever you serve at your Candlemas feast. The braid symbolizes Brigid in her aspect as the bride, which is representative of her fertility and position as a hearth goddess. Make sure you quote us on that when you bring it out to the table.

So Corny
Another notable food for this celebration is corn. In the Middle Ages, a loaf of bread and an ear of corn were left outdoors on the night of February 1st as offerings to the saint.

We've combined all three ingredients—milk, bread, and corn—into a delicious bread pudding.

Brigid's Savory Bread Pudding

With cheese, corn, and all the things necessary to celebrate Candlemas!

Ingredients

1 French baguette, about a pound
1 Tbsp each of fresh rosemary, sage, and thyme,
   finely chopped
1½ tsp salt
1½ tsp black pepper
2 large garlic cloves, minced
½ stick unsalted butter, melted
Olive oil
1 large red onion, diced
1 fennel bulb, trimmed and thinly sliced
4 cups diced mushrooms (we used baby bellas)
1 cup steamed, plain corn
3½ cups heavy cream
7 large eggs
1 tsp ground coriander
½ cup chopped, fresh parsley
1 lb white cheddar cheese; ¾ cut into small
   cubes and ¼ grated

Directions

❧ Preheat oven to 375°F. Cut the ends off of the bread, and discard or eat.

❧ Cut the loaf into bite-size pieces. In a large bowl, mix the bread, rosemary, sage, thyme, ½ teaspoon of salt, ½ teaspoon of pepper, garlic, and melted butter.

❧ Spread the bread mixture onto a baking pan and toast until golden and mildly crunchy. This takes about 20 minutes, but you should keep an eye on it to make sure that the bread chunks do not burn (it smells far too good for that to happen, anyway). Place the bread back in the bowl.

❧ Add a few tablespoons of olive oil into a large skillet and add your onion and fennel over medium heat. As they start to soften, add the mushrooms and corn. Sauté until the vegetables are soft. You may need to turn the heat up a bit to cook off the juices at the bottom of the pan. Place the cooked vegetables into the same bowl as the bread.

❧ In a separate bowl, whisk the cream, eggs, coriander, remaining portions of the salt and pepper, and parsley. Mix the wet mixture into the bread, add the cubed cheese and vegetables, and stir. We recommend that you let this sit for a half hour or more in the refrigerator. You can do this the day before if you wish, but it is not necessary. The longer you wait, the more goodness gets soaked into the delicious bread cubes.

❧ Now that you are ready, preheat the oven to 350°F. We used four individual loaf pans that were 5¾ x 3 inches; however, you can choose to do everything in a large pan. Butter the pan(s); we also lined our buttered pans with parchment paper for ease of removal.

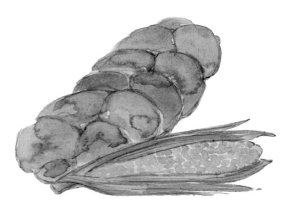

❧ It is always recommended to place your pan(s) on a cookie sheet to catch any drips. The cooking time will vary depending on your pan; we cooked them for 45 minutes.

❧ Once you see that the food has set and the top is beginning to brown, remove the bread pudding from the oven. Generously cover the top of the pudding with grated cheese.

❧ Place the pan back into the oven to melt the cheese on top. Once the cheese has melted, remove from the oven and let cool for 10–15 minutes.

St. Valentine's Day

February 14th
Eat your chickpeas.

The History

St. Valentine's official title is St. Valentinus of Rome. He was buried in the Via Flaminia near Rome on February 14th. It was officially declared St. Valentine's day by King Henry II of England.

Will the Real Valentinus Please Stand Up?
The information about his life is fairly vague, so much so that in 1969, the Roman Catholic Church removed his name from their celebrations calendar (the General Roman Calendar).

There were in fact three martyrs from the same era that all had the same name, "Valentinus." So, it's not surprising there is some confusion over who St. Valentine really was, which led to many tall tales and legends.

It is most likely that the story of St. Valentine was based on two men who were executed around the same time. The legends have combined into one theory that Valentinus was a priest that defied Emperor Claudius II, who had banned marriage as a way to keep the men in his army focused on their military missions. The young priest was caught secretly marrying couples and was sentenced to beheading for breaking the law. Children passed notes to him in prison, which may have started the concept of sending love letters. He was martyred for giving up his life to perform a holy sacrament—essentially, for loving God. The soon-to-be-without-a-head priest also cured a blind girl from behind bars and left her a message signed, "your Valentine."

This all led up to what we now celebrate on February 14th . . . love. However, St. Valentine is also the patron saint of beekeepers, epilepsy, lovers, plague, fainting, traveling, engaged couples, and happy marriages. Busy man.

The practice of sending Valentine's Day cards dates back to 1477. The love letter from Margery Brews to her fiancé, John Paston, now sits in a British museum. It is riddled with very mushy, lovey-dovey lines like, "My heart me bids evermore to love you truly over all earthly things."

Literary Love
It was most likely Chaucer who associated the feast day with love. In 1381, he wrote a poem about the engagement of Richard II and Anne of Bohemia. "For this was on St. Valentine's Day, when every bird cometh there to choose his mate."

Shakespeare nods to this day in both *Hamlet* and *A Midsummer Night's Dream*, mentioning the custom of single women sitting at their windows on February 14 with the belief that the first man who walked by would be their true love.

> Shakespeare mentioned food and drink quite a bit in his writing. In *Romeo and Juliet*, a servant in the play asks to "save me a piece of marchpane." As you could probably guess, this was the medieval version of marzipan. It was made with ground almonds, sugar, and rosewater. The marchpane was formed into elaborate shapes and used as a centerpiece for fancy dinners.

As with any feast, St. Valentine's Day is all about the food. In medieval times, young women would eat strange foods to induce dreams of their future husbands. Love spells were developed and sold in the sixteenth century. Some of these foods and spells involved eating a mixture of leeks and earthworms to strengthen a relationship, pinning bay leaves around your pillow, and throwing marigolds along your desired lover's path. With this in mind, we can see that medieval people truly believed that food could influence their love life and virility. Certain foods could provoke lust and desire, which leads us to aphrodisiacs.

"Doctors" advised those looking to improve their sex lives to consume a combination of foods that nourished and caused flatulence (described as "windy"), as well as to use ingredients that were "warm and moist." The one food having all three descriptors was chickpeas. However, goat meat, sparrow brains, and wine were also thought to have the same effect. We're sticking with chickpeas and wine, thanks.

So, back to Chaucer: original medieval Valentine's Day recipes for game bird were very popular because of the Chaucerian link between lovebirds and Valentine's Day. According to his poem "The Parliament of Foules," birds, like humans, could choose their mates. Swallows, hummingbirds, larks, pigeons, etc., were thus prepared in many ways, though mostly in pies.

As we mentioned previously, when cooking authentic medieval recipes, one must keep in mind that *many* of the ingredients we have readily available were not, in fact, in existence during that time or had not yet been discovered. For example, chocolate was not popular in the United Kingdom until the seventeenth and eighteenth centuries, so although this holiday is marked today by gifts of chocolates in heart-shaped boxes, this practice did not come about until the 1890s.

No Fruit for You!
Fresh fruit was considered to be peasant food, so the nobles rarely ate any of it unless it was in a pie or pudding. However, cherries (and dates) were considered exotic and highly sought after. Henry

VIII introduced cherries to his Kingdom after tasting them (and we're guessing he ate a *lot* of them) during a trip to Flanders.

Sealed with a Kiss!
The "X" or "kiss" we currently write at the bottom of our cards to indicate a kiss (for example, XOXO) comes from the Middle Ages—those who couldn't write their names would often sign documents with an X and kissed it to show sincerity.

Virile Chickpeas

Bold and manly, though a bit ironic that they are called "chick" peas.

Ingredients

2 Tbsp olive oil
2 cloves garlic, minced
1 Tbsp fresh rosemary, minced
Zest (1 Tbsp) and juice of one lemon (¼ cup)
2 15-oz. cans chickpeas (garbanzo beans),
    drained and rinsed
2 cups baby spinach, chopped
1 cup chicken stock
1 tsp pepper
½ tsp salt
½ cup shredded cheddar
¼ cup fresh parsley, finely chopped

Directions

- Heat the olive oil in a sauté pan on medium heat. Add the garlic and rosemary to the hot pan until fragrant and then add the lemon zest (it smells *so* good).

- Stir and add the chickpeas to the mixture. Incorporate all the ingredients and cook for 3–5 minutes.

- Stir in the lemon juice, spinach, chicken stock, pepper, and salt. Cook until the liquid is gone.

- Remove from heat, add to a serving plate, and finish with the cheddar and parsley.

"No Blackbirds" Cherry Bread Pudding

With a wee bit of booze to sweeten the deal.

Ingredients for Bread Pudding

2 cups whole milk
12 cups heavy cream
1 loaf French bread, at least a day old, cut into
   1-inch squares (about 6–7 cups)
3 eggs
2 cups sugar
2 Tbsp almond extract
¼ tsp allspice
½ tsp cinnamon
1 cup currants (soaked an hour or two in ½ cup
   Drambuie)
4 Tbsp unsalted butter, melted
11 cups cherries, chopped (please, people—not
   maraschino)

Ingredients for Drambuie Sauce

½ cup (1 stick) butter, melted
1 cup sugar
2 large eggs
1½ cups Drambuie
½ cup heavy cream

Directions for Bread Pudding

❖ Preheat your oven to 350°F.

❖ Place milk and cream in a large mixing bowl. Add the sliced bread to the milk mixture. Using your hands, press the bread into the milk and leave aside until milk is absorbed (or pretty close to being absorbed).

❖ In a separate bowl, whisk the eggs, and then add the sugar, almond extract, allspice, and cinnamon. Add the soaked currants to the egg mixture along with the remaining liquid from the Drambuie. Stir all to combine.

❖ Pour the melted butter into the bottom of a 9x13-inch baking pan. Tilt the pan to ensure that the butter gets onto the sides and in the corners. Pour the bread mixture into the pan first, followed by the milk mixture. This is when we add the cherries (the cherries go in at the end to avoid turning everything red). Ever so gently, stir the mixture together. Bake for 45 minutes, or whenever the liquid has set and the edges start to brown.

Directions for the Drambuie Sauce

❖ This is a simple *wow* recipe, but you will need to take your time. It's all about technique. On low heat, melt the butter. We prefer breaking up the butter into pats, allowing for quicker even melting. In a separate bowl, mix the sugar and eggs together. Once the butter has melted, slowly add the sugar and egg mix, and whisk gently.

❖ This is where you want to take your time. You are adding eggs to hot butter . . . you know what that means right? Cooked eggs. By cooking on low heat and slowly adding the eggs to the butter, you will hopefully avoid the "cooked egg" look. Do not let the mixture simmer or boil. You will surely have a mess on your hands.

❧ Once the mixture is thick enough to coat the back of a wooden spoon, remove from heat. Add the Drambuie and heavy cream. Stir well. Pour into a pretty jar. You are going to want to make this in advance, at least a few hours, so that the sauce will thicken up in the refrigerator.

Not So Much Lovebirds, But . . .

In 1549, an Italian cookbook contained a recipe for a pie in which live birds would fly out when the pie was cut. Shakespeare hints at the famous nursery rhyme "Sing a Song of Sixpence" in *Twelfth Night* (1602), but the actual rhyme is credited to George Stevens (1736–1800) and was published in 1744.

Sing a song of sixpence,
A pocket full of rye.
Four and twenty blackbirds,
Baked in a pie.
When the pie was opened,
The birds began to sing;
Wasn't that a dainty dish,
To set before the king?
The king was in his counting house,
Counting out his money;
The queen was in the parlor,
Eating bread and honey.
The maid was in the garden,
Hanging out the clothes,
When down came a blackbird
And pecked off her nose.

"Drunk on Love" Veal with Cherries

Love, Drambuie . . . same thing.

Ingredients

4 veal cutlets
1 Tbsp unsalted butter, plus ½ stick (chilled)
1 large shallot, diced
¾ cup chicken or veal stock
¼ cup Drambuie
1 cup cherries
1 tsp allspice

> Beautiful dark cherries are seasonal. If you cannot find them in your produce aisle, do not hesitate to look in the frozen food aisle. Just make sure your selection is not sugared. Plain cherries are what you are looking for.

Directions

- ⚜ Salt and pepper the veal cutlets.

- ⚜ Add one tablespoon of butter to a sauté pan and melt over medium heat. Sauté the veal for 3 minutes on each side. Veal cutlets can cook very quickly, resulting in toughness. We would recommend slightly undercooking and finishing the process in the cherry sauce at the end.

- ⚜ Remove the veal from the hot pan and set aside. Add the shallot and sauté for a moment, then add the stock and Drambuie. Scrape up all the lovely bits. Cook for 5 minutes.

- ⚜ Add the cherries and the allspice. Cook for another 10 minutes until the mixture is reduced by half.

- ⚜ Remove the remaining chilled butter from the refrigerator and cut into pats. While whisking the cherry mixture, add one pat of butter at a time. Once the butter has melted, lower the heat to medium low and add the veal back into the pan. Cook for 3–5 minutes.

- ⚜ Remove the veal to the serving plates; pour cherry mixture over the veal.

April Fool's Day

April 1st
Drink up, pull a prank, sit back, and enjoy the laughs.

The History
Fool's Paradise
In the 1500's, Pope Gregory XIII issued a decree stating that his new calendar (the Gregorian Calendar) be observed throughout Europe. They had previously followed the Julian calendar, in which the new year began on March 25 and was celebrated until April 1.

It had to be extremely difficult to get an enormous amount of people to switch over, but he did. April Fools was a term for those who were "foolish" enough to celebrate the New Year according to the *old* calendar. As a result, these "fools" were subject to ridicule and pranks.

Because of the confusion in the calendars, this holiday is often associated with the Feast of Fools (a New Year's celebration). During the Middle Ages, the Feast of Fools was observed as an adaptation of Saturnalia. The feast evolved into a mockery of Christianity and was, of course, prohibited by the church. However, the defiant people of the times chose to continue the revelry until the late sixteenth century.

Saturnalia was the harvest festival that honored the god, Saturn. For this celebration, all class distinctions were ignored, slaves and masters switched roles, and most laws regarding behavior were set aside (you can see where this is going).

During the medieval period, the Feast of Fools became a giant out-of-hand party. A King of Fools was elected (also referred to as the Lord of Misrule, King of Bean, the Abbot of Unreason, etc.) There was a lot of cross-dressing, heavy drinking, gambling, and other unapproved acts. Mock religious masses were held and instead of saying "Amen," the attendees gave a "hee-haw."

Catholic Kibosh

All good things must come to end, so in the sixteenth century, most of the buffoonery had been extinguished by the Catholic Church. However, as we've all come to know, it really didn't end there.

To properly honor a day that the pious medieval priests would frown upon, we suggest an extremely indulgent soup in which something isn't quite as it seems (*ale!*), paired with a lot of adult beverages. It's all about breaking the rules and testing the patience of your loved ones.

Fool's Paradise Onion Soup

The joke is on your guests, there's ALE in there! Burp.

Ingredients

4 Tbsp butter
2 Tbsp olive oil
2 pounds sweet onions, thinly sliced (we used a mandoline)
1 Tbsp sugar
1 tsp salt
2 Tbsp all-purpose flour
4 cups beef stock
1 cup chicken stock
2 bay leaves
½ to 1 cup ale
1 tsp Worcestershire sauce
2 Tbsp brown sugar
¾ cup heavy cream
French baguette
1 cup shredded white cheddar cheese

Directions

⚜ Over medium heat, melt the butter with the olive oil in a pan. Stir onions into the butter/oil mixture and leave alone for about 10 minutes. Give the onions a stir and add sugar and salt. Stir once more and let it cook until a golden brown. You may need to stir occasionally and lower the temperature to avoid burning.

⚜ Once the onions have caramelized, add the flour and stir. Cook for 2 minutes, and then add the stocks, bay leaves, ale, Worcestershire sauce, and brown sugar. Ale can create bitterness, and some people like it while others do not. If you are in the "do not" category, cook the soup longer for a good half hour to 45 minutes. Slowly add the cream and stir.

⚜ Set the oven to low broil. Cut the baguette into slices and lay them on a cookie sheet. Add the cheese to the top of the bread and put them into the oven to golden.

⚜ Ladle the soup into a bowl and lay the cheesy bread on top of the soup.

Shrove Tuesday

First Tuesday before Ash Wednesday
Celebrated for three days (Sunday through Tuesday). Summary: Who doesn't love pancakes?

The History
Pagans & Pancakes

Shrove Tuesday dates back to the Middle Ages, but, like most of the feasts mentioned in this book, it has pagan roots. The pagans made round pancakes as a symbol of the sun. The first pancake was set on a windowsill as an offering to their ancestors and leftovers were thrown in a bonfire as a sacrifice to the gods.

Throughout the world, various countries and religions mark this day by cooking pancakes, using rich and fatty ingredients before the start of Lent, during which they were required to eat plain, non-indulgent foods. Shrove Tuesday was considered the "last hoorah" before having to fast for forty days. Ingredients such as eggs, milk, fats, etc., would have to be used up so as not to go bad during the fasting period.

This day is celebrated in France (and New Orleans) as Fat Tuesday or Mardi Gras and as Carnival in South America. Other regions throughout the world celebrate with special dishes like pea soup (Poland), laskiaispulla pastry (Finland), semla (Sweden), and salted meats (Iceland); the general message being "a feast before fasting."

In Ireland, unmarried girls would flip the first pancake. If she was successful, rumor had it that she would be married within the year. In Scotland, the pancake or "bannock" was placed under a girl's pillow to induce dreams of her future husband.

For three days (Shrovetide week), giant feasts were prepared, all of which ended on Tuesday night. It was England that carried on the pagan tradition of serving pancakes and incorporated "pancake day races" where competitors dressed in aprons would run through a set course while flipping pancakes in their frying pans.

Because the Lent period was void of any sort of revelry, Shrovetide week was also a time of joy—jousting competitions, tug of war, chasing a greased pig, cockfighting (yikes), and other forms of sporty merriment would take place. In Derbyshire, England, the annual Royal Shrovetide Football Match has been played every year since 1667.

Celebrations also included "lend crocking," which is a medieval version of "trick-or-treat" where children would go door-to-door asking for pancakes. If they were refused, smashed pottery would be "anonymously" thrown at the house. Harsh!

Pagan Pancakes

With cheddar cheese, bacon jam, and crème fraîche!

- The recipe for bacon jam can be found on page 16.
- This is a savory, cheesy pancake. We love bacon jam (maybe a little too much), but you could replace it with raspberry preserves or a chutney.

Ingredients for Pancakes:

1 Tbsp unsalted butter
2 large shallots, sliced
1 Tbsp finely chopped fresh sage
1 cup all-purpose flour
1 tsp baking powder
½ tsp baking soda
½ tsp salt
1 Tbsp sugar
1 large egg, beaten
1 cup buttermilk
½ cup whole milk
1 cup grated mild cheddar
1 cup grated sharp cheddar

Other Ingredients

Bacon jam
Crème fraîche
Fresh, chopped sage

Directions

- In a small sauté pan, heat the butter and add the shallots and fresh sage. This will brown and soften quickly, even on medium heat, so keep a good eye on this.

- Remove from heat and allow to cool. In a large mixing bowl, add the dry ingredients (flour, baking powder, baking soda, salt, and sugar), and combine.

- Add the egg, buttermilk, and milk to the dry ingredients. Mix thoroughly, removing all lumps. Add the cooled shallots and sage, and mix. Then add the cheese and fully incorporate in the mixing bowl. Set the mixture aside for 20 minutes.

- Heat skillet or griddle. Add butter to the hot pan. These pancakes can be made as a meal or an appetizer—we made this as an appetizer using square metal molds/biscuit/cookie cutters.

Presentation

- Place a pancake on a plate. Add a scoop of bacon jam on the top, followed with a plop of crème fraîche. Finish with fresh chopped sage.

Easter

Celebrated in March/April

Sacrifice and celebrate. Sacrifice and celebrate.

The History

Food at Last! Thank God We Have Food at Last!

Easter was the most important holiday in the medieval calendar, primarily because of its religious ties, as you can probably guess. Although Easter Sunday was the main focus, the Easter "season" was about 120 days long and included periods of fasting as well as feasting. The days leading up to Easter Sunday were called the Triduum—Maundy Thursday, Good Friday, and Holy Saturday. During the Triduum, religious services were almost completely in the dark and the mood was quite solemn. However, on Easter Sunday the services (starting at dawn) would be joyful, hopeful, and bright.

And Then There's That Creepy Hare Thing

Traditions included Pace eggs—hard boiled eggs decorated with flower and vegetable dyes and often capped with lace, jewels, or family crests. The Pace eggs were often used as gifts and were hidden for children to find, much like today. The first mention of the Easter Bunny doesn't appear until 1682—this began as a German tradition. The Easter Bunny would determine if children were well-behaved, leaving eggs for the kiddos who met his standards.

Lent (the period leading up to Easter) was definitely a time of fasting. After forty days of eating very little (and nothing that could've possibly tasted good), you can believe that the joyous feast of Easter was something to marvel at (as your belly growled).

Another tradition for this day was new clothes! For some, this was the only time of the year when they would actually receive a new piece of clothing. In the courts, kings and queens would give their own clothes to some of their servants, and perhaps even cattle as an added bonus. Most of the time these gifts were politically motivated, but it's nice to think that one or two did it out of gratitude and kindness.

We Know You Are *Dye-ing* to Try This

To make a natural medieval-ish dye for your eggs, you can use red onion peels, beets, red cabbage, turmeric, blueberries, or even tea. We recommend the onion skins, but all yield amazing results that you can experiment with.

You will need:

12 onions skins, the dry part (you can use regular or red onions)
3 Tbsp vinegar
1 dozen eggs, room temperature

Boil about 5 cups of water in a stainless steel pot, and add the dry skin of the onions (only the skin) and the vinegar. After it boils, let it simmer for 20 minutes. Remove and let cool.

When it reaches room temperature, strain the mixture to remove any skin pieces. Arrange eggs in your pot and pour colored water over the eggs. Bring everything to a boil, reduce heat, and cover. Keep checking your color results. It should not take more than 10–15 minutes.

You can try this with any of the items we mentioned—rhubarb and saffron also work very well.

Simnel Cake (on the left plate) is a traditional Easter dish that dates back *way* before the medieval times. It is essentially a fruitcake with almond paste. But don't worry, we wouldn't do that to you.

During the reign of Elizabeth I, the sale of hot cross buns (on the right plate) was forbidden except for use at burials, Good Friday, or Christmas. "Good Friday comes this month, the old woman runs. With one or two a penny, hot cross buns."

"Silence of the Lambs" Stew

Don't get any on your new Easter outfit!

Ingredients

5 Tbsp olive oil
2 yellow onions, thinly sliced
3 carrots, sliced
3½–4 lb lamb meat, trimmed and cubed (we used boneless leg of lamb)
1 cup all-purpose flour
1 tsp cinnamon, plus ½ tsp during cooking process
1 tsp salt
1 tsp black ground pepper
½ stick unsalted butter
4 cups beef stock
3 garlic cloves, minced
2 Tbsp peeled and minced fresh ginger
1 cup chopped dates
Grated zest of 2 medium lemons (about 4 tablespoons)
1 15-oz. can chickpeas, rinsed and drained
2 Tbsp finely chopped fresh flat-leaf parsley
1 Tbsp chopped fresh mint
Plain Greek yogurt

Directions

❧ In a Dutch oven over medium heat, warm 2 Tbsp of the olive oil. Add the onions and sauté until softened, about 5 minutes. Add the carrots and cook until slightly softened, about 3 minutes more. Transfer to a bowl and set aside.

❧ Pat the lamb dry with paper towels. Place the flour in a sealable plastic bag and season with cinnamon, salt, and pepper. Add the lamb in batches and stir or shake to coat thoroughly with the seasoned flour.

❧ Warm the remaining 3 Tbsp of oil in the pot over medium-high heat. Working in batches to avoid crowding, add the lamb and brown on all sides, 4 to 5 minutes for each batch. You may need to add additional oil as necessary, to prevent from burning.

❧ Keep the remaining flour in the bag for later use; there should be approximately ¼ cup of seasoned flour left. Transfer the cooked meat to a bowl and set aside.

❧ Preheat the oven to 350°F. In the Dutch oven, melt the butter and add the remaining flour from the bag. Stir until thick, a few minutes. Add the stock and bring to a boil, stirring with a wooden spoon to scrape up the browned bits from the bottom.

❧ Add the garlic, ½ tsp cinnamon, and ginger. Return the onion mixture and the lamb along with any accumulated juices to the pot. Add the dates, lemon zest, and chickpeas, and bring to a boil over high heat.

❧ Once it has reached boiling temperature, cover the pot, transfer to the oven, and bake until the meat is tender, 1½ to 2 hours. Right before serving, stir in the parsley and mint. Serve the stew with a dollop of yogurt.

Onion and Cheese Tarts

No creepy rabbits, just veggies.

Ingredients

1 cup heavy cream
1¼ tsp lavender (use cooking approved
  lavender, not the stuff in bags in your closet)
2 medium sweet onions, thinly sliced
½ tsp salt
1 Tbsp honey
½ lb Double Gloucester cheese with blue Stilton,
  crumbled (if you cannot find this combination,
  buy the items separately and crumble
  together)
8 large eggs
Piecrust (page 18; you can use store-bought, but
  homemade is better)

Directions

- Heat the heavy cream and lavender together over low heat until it warms, not boils. Shut the heat off and allow the ingredients to infuse for 10 minutes. Strain and discard the lavender. Set the cream aside.

- We made four individual pies, using the piecrust recipe on page 18 and individual springform pans. However, you can use a single crust if you wish. We will say that the individual pies are perfect for a brunch or a single portion. Whatever you choose, preheat the oven to 350°F.

- Mix the onions, salt, honey, cheese, and eggs together. Gently mix. Add the lavender-infused cream and stir. Pour the mixture into the crust of choice. If you have any extra cheese, sprinkle the crumble onto the top of the mixture.

- Place the pan(s) on a cookie sheet to capture any spillage. Cook for 50 minutes (individual) to 60 minutes for a larger size. You may need to adjust the cooking time depending on your oven. Look for a firm center and a golden top.

Hocktide

Celebrated the second Monday and Tuesday after Easter.
A little Fifty-Shades-of-Grey-ish, but hey . . . cheesy bread!

The History

Hocktide, along with Michaelmas, divided the rural agricultural calendar into winter and summer. Hocktide was a very important day in late medieval England.

I'm All Tied Up at the Moment

On Monday, men would tie women up with ropes and only release them for a fee (we kid you not), and on Tuesday the women would tie the men up with ropes and release them for a fee. It was a medieval fund-raiser! All money collected was donated to the local church.

Hocktide celebrations date back to the twelfth century. However, Henry VIII vehemently banned all talk of Hocktide. His daughter Elizabeth reinstated the party upon her visit to Kenilworth Castle in 1575. There in Kenilworth, kisses were taken as payment for releasing whomever was tied up instead of money.

All of this Fifty-Shades-of-Grey stuff is thought to commemorate the torture the English endured by the Danes in the ninth century. It was also a day for paying rent and debts, hence the phrase "in hock," which refers to owing money.

The celebration of Hocktide faded in the seventeenth century but is still celebrated in Hungerford, England, where they have nicknamed it "Tutti Day." The original reason the people of Hungerford celebrated Hocktide was in honor of their great patron, John of Gaunt (1430–1399), who granted the town special hunting and fishing rights. To this day, Tutti Men visit local homes accompanied by six local Tutti girls and collect kisses from each lady in the house. Sounds a little creepy, but they seem to have fun with it.

The festive people of Hungerford celebrate every year with macaroni and cheese with watercress, Welsh rarebit, or anchovies on toast . . . and an ale tasting, of course.

Welsh Rarebit

Also known as hot, oozing cheesy bread.

Ingredients

One small French baguette
1 Tbsp olive oil
1 clove garlic, finely diced and mashed
4 Tbsp butter
4 Tbsp flour
¾ cup mead
6 ounces Stilton cheese—cut up 5 ounces into
    medium-size pieces; reserve approximately an
    ounce to the side, which should be in smaller,
    crumbled pieces
1½ Tbsp Dijon mustard
2 dashes Worcestershire sauce
6 figs (we selected Mission figs)

> Welsh rarebit is simply a dish made with
> a savory cheese and served hot over
> toasted bread. Although that "official"
> name didn't appear until the early 1700s,
> the first reference to "caws pobi" (Welsh
> for toasted cheese) appears in a fourteenth
> century text.

Directions

⚜ Cut the baguette in half, lengthwise. Mix together the olive oil and garlic. Using a pastry brush, paint the olive oil and garlic onto the baguette and lightly toast in the oven.

⚜ While the bread is toasting, add the butter to a saucepan, on medium heat, until melted. Slowly sprinkle in the flour, stirring constantly. Once the butter and flour are incorporated, pour in the mead. Stir until smooth.

⚜ Add the Stilton chunks, stirring often, until melted. Add the Dijon, followed by the Worcestershire sauce. The consistency will be thick and will not stick to the pan; it will be almost paste-like with a buttery appearance.

⚜ Turn the oven to low broil. Cut the figs into slices and lay them onto the toasted bread. Spoon the cheese mixture over the top of the figs and finish it by sprinkling the remaining one ounce of crumbled Stilton over the top. Tuck into the oven, top rack, and watch carefully. It will only take 8–10 minutes, but, depending on your oven, it can go more or less. You know how that goes.

⚜ Once the cheese begins to bubble and starts to get golden on the top, remove from the oven and rest. This is *hot* so don't be tempted to cut and eat immediately. Hello, hot molten cheese people!

⚜ **On a selfish note**: If you are like us and love eating the cheese that melts onto the pan and gets that super crunchy taste—don't make this with a friend that likes the same. They will grab it from you and claim victory. Save those for yourself. (We *may* be speaking from experience.)

Rogation Days

Major Rogation, April 25th
Bless your crops, keep the revelry to a minimum . . . or not.

The History

The first rogation days ceremonies presumably took place in the seventh century, with a first appearance in a twelfth century text. This was a day to observe a change in the season and begin spring planting. There are four rogation days, with the "Major" being on April 25. The purpose was to ask God to bless the fields and the church.

Meet Me at the Altar

A procession route was established along the boundaries of the church where the parishioners would walk carrying banners, crosses, and bells to mark the parish perimeter. They would speak with neighbors and ask God and the saints to bless crops (wheat, peas, beans, oats), livestock, and their fishing expeditions. In return, they promised to give to the poor and needy. How sweet!

Medieval kings and queens celebrated the major rogation days with a "Royal Entry," a procession in which the king or queen (or other royalty) would follow the procession route, be greeted by their people along the way, and then

be welcomed to various parishes with appropriate homage and a feast. Sometimes, several altars would be built along their route for prayers.

This holiday, too, became a bit "wild." Although it was officially ordered that all attend and observe the rogation days, the festivities got so out of control with drinking and revelry that the church elders encouraged local priests to only invite pious men. This problem was most notable during the reign of King Henry VIII. What a buzzkill. Soon after, the rogation procession became a sort of "hushed" event, only returning to the public limelight when Elizabeth I became queen. We like to call her the "Fun Queen."

Sauce Madame, for the Fun Queen

A saucy chicken dish to share with your Kingdom.

Ingredients

3 lb boneless, skinless chicken thighs
1 cup flour
3 tsp sea salt (we like fleur de sel)
3 tsp black pepper
1 Tbsp olive oil
4 Tbsp unsalted butter
2 cloves garlic, thinly sliced
1 large onion, thinly sliced (we used
    sweet yellow)
2 pears, quartered and thinly sliced
2 cups red seedless grapes
5 sprigs fresh thyme
2 Tbsp quince paste (quince paste
    has the added bonus of lemon and
    sugar, and it is easier to find than
    quince)
1 cup Riesling, or a sweet wine
2 cups chicken stock
1 tsp cinnamon
1 tsp of ginger
½ tsp nutmeg
½ cup chopped fresh parsley

Directions

- Remove excess fat from the chicken and discard. In a shallow mixing bowl, add flour, 2 tsp of salt, and 2 tsp of black pepper. Mix and add chicken. Coat completely.

- Add the olive oil and 2 Tbsp of butter in an appropriate pan to braise. Melt the butter over medium heat, and, once hot, add the chicken. Turn after 2–3 minutes, each side. We used a heavy copper pan so 3 minutes was better for us, but if your pan is lighter 2 minutes may be appropriate. The moral of that story . . . just watch your chicken.

- Remove chicken and set aside. Add the remaining butter to the pan. Add the garlic first and cook until fragrant, followed by the onion. Once the onion begins to soften, add the pears. You may need to add some additional butter at this point. Gently stir after a few minutes, and then add the grapes and sprigs of thyme.

- Cook until the grapes become warm. Visually, you will be able to see when the grapes get warm when, like us, they start to sweat. Scoop out the quince paste and add it to the pan. Gently stir (you don't want to damage the fruit). Then, add the Riesling and chicken stock.

- The next ingredients to go into this beautiful pan are the spices: cinnamon, ginger, nutmeg, and the remaining salt and pepper. Stir and turn the pan up to high to get it to a rolling boil. Move the dial down to medium low—low and slow.

- Place each piece of chicken back in to the pan. Add only one at a time and nudge each piece of chicken to get them cuddled up to the fruit and vegetables.

- Cover the pan tightly and cook for 15 minutes. Do your best not to open the lid; patience. After 15 minutes, remove the lid, flip the chicken over, and, using a wooden spoon, scrape up any food that is sticking to the bottom.

- Cook covered for another 20 minutes. Repeat the chicken flip and cook for a final 20 minutes, again covered. Salt and pepper to taste. Add the fresh parsley. Serve with a delicious loaf of bread—the sauce is too good not to mop up.

Medieval Wedding

Dowries, gifts, mead, and merrymaking.

The History

Who doesn't love a wedding? Well, sometimes being a bridesmaid is a bit of a nightmare, but still . . . Medieval weddings were an outdoor event where the church was decorated with banners and candles (or torches). Weddings were primarily, as you can imagine, arranged. These arrangements were most often politically motivated or for social advancement. It was rare for a woman to even know her future husband before the wedding, and, in most cases, he would be a *lot* older than she was.

No one wore white. White was the color of mourning (not morning). It was more traditional to wear blue as a symbol of purity (this is where the "something blue" tradition originates from). Peasants simply wore the best garment they owned, no matter what color it was. Rings, dowries, gifts, and garters were all part of a medieval wedding. Unfortunately, the wording of vows is almost exactly the same. (What? Clearly this needs updating.) And here's something rather amusing—the "best man" referred to the "best swordsman." This swordsman was responsible for ensuring that no one disrupted the wedding!

The ceremony took place outside the church before the nuptial Mass. When they did go inside for the Mass, the groom stood on the right and the bride to the left, both facing the door of the church.

After the ceremony, guests would gather for a feast. There was no ten-foot-tall flower-covered cake for the bride and groom; however, medieval wedding feasts had more food than most of the guests would've seen in a year. Menus consisted almost entirely of meat, fish, eels, and oysters, along with dairy products such as cheese and butter.

Guests remained at the wedding until all the food was consumed, and the wine gone. We may know a few houseguests like that. Ahem.

I Do, I Do, I Do Scallops with Pea Puree

A delicate dish for delicate situations.

Ingredients

1 Tbsp unsalted butter
1 clove garlic
2 fresh mint leaves
1 cup sweet peas, thawed if you have frozen
  peas
½ cup chicken stock
2 Tbsp grated cheese (we used pecorino)
3 Tbsp mascarpone
Salt and pepper, to taste
6–8 large scallops
Unsalted butter and olive oil for searing

> We like U10 or any large "dry" scallops.
> "Dry packed" means that the scallops are
> not artificially enlarged with water (or
> worse, chemicals). If you are spending the
> money on fresh seafood, spend it wisely.

Directions for the Puree

- In a saucepan, heat butter on medium heat until melted. Add the garlic and mint. This will be incredibly aromatic. Once the garlic softens, not browns, add the peas and chicken stock.

- When the peas warm and soften, add the cheese and stir. Using a hand mixer or blender, puree the pea mixture until smooth.

- Add the puree back onto the heat, medium low, and then add the mascarpone. Salt and pepper to taste.

Directions for the Scallops

- Pat the scallops dry, and remove any remaining muscles with your fingers. Generously sprinkle the scallops with salt and pepper. Swirl olive oil around the pan. The pan should be big enough to fit all your scallops comfortably.

- Heat the pan over medium-to-medium-high heat. Place the scallops on the hot pan. The secret to searing scallops is to leave them alone! Allowing 3–4 minutes for each side will brown the scallops nicely.

- This is an optional technique that yields delicious results. Once you flip the scallops over to cook on the other side, add a few pats of cold, unsalted butter. This gives the scallops a nice finish and a golden color to the serving side. You can also, when adding the butter, incorporate fresh herb or spice. Our favorite spice with scallops is ground coriander.

- Place the scallops on a plate, buttered side up, with the pea puree. You can serve the scallops beside the puree or serve over. Your preference. We did scallops on the puree, with a bit of mint sprinkled on top.

May Day

May 1st

Get your flower crown on and dance, dance, dance, but beware of moth attacks.

The History

Don't Tell the Priest Where We're Going

May Day celebrated the end of winter. It was a promise of things to come—spring and summer, harvest, good weather, and food!

The celebrations began the night before when everyone would gather around the bonfire to dance, drink, sing, and eat. They shared stories of previous years' festivities and genuinely enjoyed themselves. On the eve of May Day, the party goers would all go out and gather flowers and branches; however, the church deemed these late night forages for foliage to be way too tempting for lust-filled young folk, so the gathering was rescheduled for daylight hours.

Oh, do not tell the Priest our plight,

Or he would call it a sin;

But we have been out in the woods all night,

A-conjuring Summer in!

The maypole was placed in the center of the village as the main feature of the day. Long woven garlands of flowers and leaves draped from the pole while the children danced in circular patterns to weave these glorious flowers into spectacular patterns. La-ti-dah.

A "Queen of May" was chosen from the local young (and single) ladies, and she was given a special crown woven together with spring flowers and branches. And, like April Fools' Day, a "Lord of Misrule" also wandered about playing the mischief-maker.

Also customary on this day—*no work*. Farm and land owners would supply large feasts for their tenants and workers. Special ale was made to toast their accomplishments and the end of a long winter. Be sure to tell that to your boss when you call in.

Faeries and Drunks Like Mugwort

Beltane is essentially the same thing as May Day, and comes from ancient Irish mythology. It is one of the four Gaelic seasonal celebrations: Samhain, Imbolc, Beltane, and Lughnassadh. The ancient Celts would perform rituals to protect their farms, livestock, and families. One of these rituals was to leave food and milk on the doorstep as an offering to the faeries.

In Romania, this day is called Mugwort Day or Drunkard's Day. Between the amount of mugwort-flavored wine consumed, the fiddlers, and the roasted lamb, we'd say the Romanians win! Mugwort is a "magical" herb that was believed to cast out demonic possessions, prevent moth attacks, ward off wild woodland beasts, and alleviate fatigue. If you plant it in your garden you can expect a visit from the good faeries. This multipurpose herb was also used in the making of absinthe as it is very similar to wormwood. There are still home brewers throughout Europe that use this licorice-flavored herb to enhance their beer.

Wet Your Whistle

Elderflowers are from the elder tree (*Sambucus nigra*). They are native to Britain. Elderflowers have small white petals that give off a very strong, sweet smell. It blooms in the months of May and June and has become a symbol of the arrival of spring. This powerful plant has been used for a number of remedies since the Middle Ages. It can be used as an anti-inflammatory, to lower a fever, to soothe rashes, and most importantly to make liqueur for cocktails (ahem . . . also a remedy). All parts of this plant are useful: bark, flowers, leaves.

There are several brands of elderflower liqueur and syrup. For the liqueur, we recommend St. Germain. They happen to pick their elderflowers in the French Alps and the elegant bottle looks gorgeous on the table.

If you do purchase a bottle for the following recipe, the rest will not go to waste. We suggest you add a tiny bit to your champagne. Just a smidge. Very fancy and delicious.

"Spring Has Sprung" Cheesecake

Decadent and divine, goes well with wine (but what doesn't?).

- This recipe creates a loaf cake first. You can eat this as is with your tea in the morning, or you can continue with the recipe and make an amazing crust for your cheesecake.
- This can be made hours or days in advance. In fact, the longer it has to stay, the better.
- When your gingerbread crust and cheesecake are all assembled (that is, if there's any left at this point), drizzle with the cinnamon-honey caramel sauce. Oh, happy day!

Ingredients for Gingerbread Crust

1 cup honey
1 loaf bread, either a few days old or dried in the oven
1 Tbsp ginger
½ Tbsp cinnamon
¼ tsp white pepper
¼ tsp ground cloves

Directions for Gingerbread Crust

- ⚜ Clarify the honey by heating it in a saucepan. Remove any foam. Trim the loaf of bread to remove the crust.

- ⚜ Add the bread, in stages, to the food processor until the bread is finely ground. While the machine is on, add the spices and then drizzle the honey into the mixture. Make sure that the mixture is thoroughly mixed and you are not seeing any resemblance to bread. Just wait until you smell the spices—amazing!

- ⚜ Line a brownie/square cake pan with wax or parchment paper. Pour the mixture into the pan and press it down firmly and evenly. We used a tart press to help with this process. Fold wax paper over the top of the cake until completely covered. Put something heavy on top of the cake and keep it in a cool, dry place for a few hours or overnight. This is not your grandmother's version of gingerbread. This is a strangely textured but delicious cake.

Ingredients for Cinnamon-Honey Caramel Sauce

1 cup honey
1 cup water
1 cup sugar
½ tsp cinnamon
1 stick unsalted butter, broken up into Tbsp sizes
1 cup heavy cream
2 tsp sea salt

Ingredients for Cheesecake

½ cup flour
1 stick butter, melted
1 Tbsp honey
2 lb cream cheese, softened to room
  temperature
1 cup white sugar, plus 1 Tbsp
4 large eggs
¼ cup whole milk
2 tsp elderflower syrup, plus ½ tsp (you can use
  elderflower liqueur)
1 cup sour cream

Directions for Cinnamon-Honey Caramel Sauce

⚜ When making this sauce, make sure that you can access it easily during the cooking process. If not, you will have an awful mess to clean up if it bubbles over.

⚜ In a heavy saucepan, add the honey, water, and sugar. Give it a stir and turn the heat on to medium. Cook for about 30 minutes until you can see it coat the back of a wooden spoon. You may need to lower the heat to low if it begins to bubble up.

⚜ Once the syrup has been reduced, remove from heat. Try not to stir too much. Add the cinnamon and stir. Add it back over medium heat and begin to add the pats of butter, one at a time, whisking it until it is melted and all the butter is gone.

⚜ Gently drizzle heavy cream into the mixture, stirring continuously as you pour. Take your time pouring the cream.

⚜ Lower the heat to low and let simmer for 5 minutes. Remove from heat, and add the salt and stir. The salt will take away some of the sweetness and make it taste more like butterscotch. Pour the cooled caramel into a pretty container and store in the refrigerator.

Directions for the Cheesecake

⚜ Preheat the oven to 325°F.

⚜ Remove gingerbread from pan. Put the gingerbread in a food processor and break down into pieces. Add ½ cup of flour and incorporate. While the machine is on, drizzle melted butter into the bowl. Immediately add honey and mix until it resembles sand.

⚜ Pour out ingredients into a prepared (buttered) 9-inch springform pan. This is where technique is important. Take your time and firmly press the ingredients into the bottom and sides of the pan. Pay close attention to the corners as they tend to be forgotten.

⚜ For the filling, put the cream cheese into a mixing bowl. Turn the mixer on medium-high and let it do its thing for a few minutes. Thoroughly whip that cream cheese good; you don't want to see any lumps! Gently add in the sugar and beat until combined with the cream cheese and very smooth.

❧ Crack the eggs into a separate bowl. With the mixer on, slowly beat in the eggs one at a time. Stop the mixing between eggs to scrape down splatter on the sides of the bowl. Also, pay attention to the very bottom of your mixing bowl; sometimes the cream cheese gets stuck there, so move your mixer around to prevent that. Turn it on again and add in the milk and the 2 tsp elderflower.

❧ Keep beating until there are no lumps. Pour mixture (without eating it) into the prepared gingerbread crust. We always place our springform pan onto a cookie sheet, in case there are any leaks. Place it in the oven for about one hour. While you are waiting for your cake to finish, combine the sour cream, 1 Tbsp of sugar, and ½ tsp of elderflower in a small bowl.

❧ After an hour, the cheesecake will still have some jiggle to it, which is the way it should be. Remove from the oven, but keep your oven on. Let the cake cool for 10 minutes, and then gently add the sour cream mixture to the top of the cake. Put it back in the oven for another 10 minutes. Remove from the oven and let it cool completely. Store it in the refrigerator, covered, for at least 6 hours. Overnight is better.

St. George's Day

April 23rd
Slay your dragons, eat something British.

The History

St. George's Day is celebrated in many countries around the world, but it is most notably recognized in England. This was a major feast in the medieval calendar since the early fifteenth century—as important as Christmas!

In 1348, St. George became the patron saint of England (among many other things), and in 1415 a national holiday was declared. Celebrations waned in the eighteenth century, but smaller festivals still remain. George was venerated as a warrior saint during the Third Crusade (1189–1192). The red cross is associated with the mysterious Knights Templar and was used by leaders or nobility who wanted to associate themselves with the crusades.

The St. George's flag was proudly carried by John Cabot on his voyage to discover Newfoundland in 1497, and in 1620 it was flown on the foremast of the *Mayflower* on its journey to Plymouth, Massachusetts.

Traditions for this day included wearing a red rose in one's lapel and flying the St. George's flag anywhere and everywhere possible.

Dragon Slayer

St. George, before being canonized, was a Roman soldier in the third century. He was a favorite of Emperor Diocletian, that is, until George spoke out publicly against the emperor and his cruelty towards Christians. This defiance against the emperor on behalf of his faith led to his eventual martyrdom.

According to legend, he was also a dragon slayer. During his life (again, this is just a legend), he came across a small town in what we now call Libya. A hermit told him that the town was being terrorized by a dragon (no, that's not a typo—a dragon). The hermit went on to say that the King of Egypt would give his daughter in marriage to the one who could put an end to the monster, and St. George accepted the challenge. When he had found the dragon, St. George attacked with his spear, but its scales were too hard. He then rolled under an enchanted orange tree that protected him from the angry dragon with its magical healing powers. St. George eventually slew the dragon by stabbing it, and was hailed as the ultimate hero or, uh, saint.

Random history: Henry VIII is buried in the St. George's Chapel in Windsor Castle.

Dragon Lamb Wellington

A very British appetizer.

Ingredients

2 Tbsp olive oil
⅓ cup red onion, minced
2 cloves garlic, minced
1 lb ground lamb
1 Tbsp fresh sage, minced
Salt and pepper, to taste
2 Tbsp unsalted butter
2 cups mushrooms, minced
½ tsp ground ginger
½ cup fresh parsley, chopped
Egg roll wrappers
1 large egg, beaten
½ lb Double Gloucester cheese with Blue Stilton
Cooking oil or lard, amount depends on size of
   pan

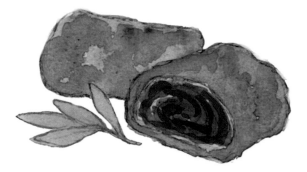

Directions

✤ In a sauté pan, heat the olive oil and add the red onion and garlic until soft. Add the ground lamb and sage, and add salt and pepper to taste. Using a wooden spoon, stir the lamb to avoid any large pieces of meat so that it cooks evenly. Once the meat is cooked, set the pan aside.

✤ Using another pan, heat 2 tablespoons of butter and add the mushrooms, ginger, and parsley. Once the mushrooms are soft and the liquid has evaporated, set the pan aside to cool.

✤ On a flat surface, spread out an egg roll wrapper. Try to remove one wrapper at a time from their packaging as the wrappers will get dry if they sit out for too long. Brush the egg along all the edges of the wrapper.

✤ In the lower center of your wrapper, add two teaspoons of the lamb, 1 teaspoon of the mushroom, and slice of cheese. Tuck the sides of the wrapper in, then roll the wrapper around the meat and seal with the egg. Repeat. Heat lard (which we recommend) or cooking oil in a deep pan. You want to place enough cooking liquid to go halfway up the center of a rolled-up egg roll.

✤ Once the cooking liquid is hot (to determine this, put the end of a dry wooden spoon in the oil; if tiny bubbles appear, it is hot enough for you to use), gently place a few of the egg rolls in the oil. Do not overcrowd them, and stay close to the pan as they fry. This will not take long.

✤ Flip the egg rolls over once they have browned. Repeat until all the rolls are cooked. Serve warm.

The Bard's Chicken Pie with Bacon Lattice

Bacon. Need we say more?

Pie Ingredients

2 pounds boneless, skinless chicken thighs
8–10 cups water
1 tsp salt, plus more for the poaching process
2 sprigs rosemary
2 sprigs thyme
5 large eggs
3 Tbsp lemon juice, fresh please
¾ tsp pepper
1 tsp ginger, dried
¼ tsp cinnamon
9-inch piecrust, deep dish
1 pound bacon

Directions

⚜ Poach chicken in 8–10 cups water, salt, rosemary, and thyme over medium to medium low heat. You want to move the cooking process along, not finish cooking them in the water.

⚜ Remove the chicken, and discard the rosemary and thyme. Once slightly cooled, cut the chicken into bite-size bites and add the chicken to a large mixing bowl. Add the eggs, lemon juice, pepper, salt, ginger, and cinnamon to the mixing bowl. Stir and combine. Pour the mixture into the prepared crust.

⚜ Preheat oven to 400°F.

❧ Apply the bacon to the top in a lattice pattern. It's a matter of weaving the bacon in an over/under pattern: place half of the bacon, side by side, vertically on the pie. Starting with the strip on the left, lift every other strip and fold it back until an inch of the bacon strips remain on the pie. From the remaining quantity of bacon, place one bacon strip horizontally across the vertical strips. Try your best to line it up nicely. Unfold the pieces of bacon over the new horizontal strip you just applied. Now, repeat the process by folding back the other vertical pieces of bacon that have yet to be folded, and insert the next horizontal strip; and repeat. Bing bang boom . . . you are done! We used kitchen shears to cut any overlapping pieces of bacon. (This sounds much harder than it actually is to make. You got it and you will look like a pro once it is done. Let's face it, no one is going to call you out on a mistake because—*bacon.*)

❧ Place the finished masterpiece on top of a cookie sheet so that it can catch any drippings from the bacon or pie. Cook the pie for 20 minutes in the oven, uncovered. After 20 minutes, baste the pie with the honey mustard, while still in the oven, doing this every 10 minutes for another 30 minutes. Total cooking time is about an hour.

Honey Mustard Glaze Ingredients

½ cup honey
1 oz dried mustard powder
3 Tbsp red wine
⅛ tsp cinnamon
⅛ tsp ginger
1 tsp red wine vinegar

Odd tidbit: William Shakespeare was born on April 23, 1564, and he died on the same day in 1616.

Honey Mustard Glaze Directions

❧ Place honey in a deep saucepan on low heat. Skim off any foam. Add the mustard and stir quickly, making the best effort to fully incorporate. Remove from heat and add the red wine, cinnamon, ginger, and red wine vinegar. Add back onto the heat until all ingredients are well blended.

Cooper's Hill Cheese Roll

The last Monday in May
Summary: Roll your cheese. Chase your cheese. Eat your cheese.

The History

Say Cheese!
Brockworth is a lovely village located in Gloucestershire, England. Every year since the fifteenth century (although most written records indicate the nineteenth century), the villagers of Brockworth have had a cheese rolling contest on Cooper's Hill. Large, round wheels of cheese are rolled down the very steep hill and chased by *extremely* competitive runners. It's funny they call them "runners" because there is more rolling, tumbling, and very awkward falls than actual running. This event draws in people from around the globe and is held every May during the spring bank holiday that falls on a Monday.

There are theories that the origins of the event tie back to pagan rituals for celebrating the arrival of summer. Large rolls of hay were lit on fire and sent down the very same hill in Brockworth. Hay on fire seems a wee bit more dangerous. We're glad this Olympic-caliber event evolved into a cheese wheel. To be perfectly honest, food is about the only thing we'd chase.

The people in charge of this event are very specific about their cheese—it has to be a Double Gloucester cheese. Double Gloucester is a traditional, semi-hard cheese which, as you can guess, is made locally in Gloucestershire. It has been made there since the sixteenth century. There are several theories as to why this cheese is called a "Double" (choose your favorite): because the milk had to be skimmed twice, because the cream from the morning milk was added to the evening milk, or because the roll is typically twice the height of other cheeses.

Cheese was quite popular throughout the Middle Ages, and there were more varieties than you'd think. For the poorer folk, cheese was their major source of protein. Cheddar, Parmesan, Brie, ricotta, and Gouda were all readily available.

Side note: During WWII, a fake cheese wheel that was made of wood was used for the race because laws banned the use of cheese in an event. Cheese was a rationed food item, so waste not, want not.

Chase That Cheese and Egg Soup

After you roll down the hill, you'll need something tasty to mend the wounds.

Ingredients

6 cups chicken stock
2 Tbsp butter
1 garlic clove, minced
1 leek, trimmed and sliced into ½-inch pieces
1 carrot, peeled and sliced thin
1 cup mushrooms, sliced
¼ tsp white pepper
¼ tsp ground ginger
¼ tsp salt
½ cup grated cheddar
2 Tbsp fresh parsley, finely chopped
3 large eggs

Directions

❧ Add the chicken stock to a medium size saucepan. In a separate pan, melt the butter and sauté the garlic, leek, carrot, and mushrooms.

❧ On medium high heat, cook the chicken stock and add the sautéed vegetables, pepper, ginger, and salt. You will want the soup to get to a rolling boil.

❧ While you are waiting for the soup to heat, place cheese, parsley, and eggs (no shells, of course) in a bowl and fully incorporate. We recommend using a bowl that is smaller than the saucepan.

❧ Once the soup has started a rolling boil, lower the heat to medium low. Using a wooden spoon, stir the soup in a continuous circular motion. With your other hand, lower and tilt the bowl of the egg mixture toward the saucepan, keeping the rim of the bowl as close as you can to the boiling soup. Slowly (and we mean slowly) stream the egg mixture into the moving soup. Continue until all the egg mixture is gone.

❧ This soup has very delicate flavors and will be delicious with a warm, savory piece of focaccia bread.

St. John's Eve/Midsummer's Eve

Celebrated between June 21st and June 25th

Get the bonfire going and dance, but don't forget your wort.

The History

Midsummer's Eve (or St. John's Eve for the Christians) is an ancient festival celebrating the summer solstice. Bonfires were lit to ward off bad spirits and drive out dragons!

In the fourteenth century, celebrations took a sinister turn—it was thought this was a powerful night for witches to congregate. It was also believed by the church that the merrymaking was completely out of hand (a bit of a trend in these times), so they ordered their parishioners to see it as a day of fasting and *not* gluttony.

The name "St. John's Eve" refers to St. John the Baptist's birth. According to the Gospel of Luke, John was born six months before Jesus, and it is one of the very few saint feast days that commemorates a birth as opposed to a death.

Evil Plants? Really?

In many parts of the world, women would collect plants on this night—fennel, rosemary, foxgloves, elderflowers, and, as you probably guessed, St. John's wort. Since before medieval times, this plant was believed to ward off evil. Branches were hung over doorways and windows for protection not only from evil but also from witches. Cackle.

Which brings us to St. John's Day in New Orleans. Many NOLA residents still celebrate this night with voodoo rituals, all of which began with the famous voodoo priestess, Marie Laveau. She held all of her most important rituals on this night in the 1800s. We could do a whole book on New Orleans food, but while we're on the subject, if you're ever down there check out the Erin Rose on 811 Conti Street, order a beer, head straight to the back, and order a po' boy.

Goody Goody

Back to medieval food—this holiday was marked by a dish called "goody" (mostly in Ireland). It was nothing more than basic white bread soaked in hot milk and flavored with sugar and spices. Hmm . . . sounds like bread pudding, right? Villagers would make this "goody" in large pots at the communal St. John's Eve bonfire. Anyone celebrating or attending the bonfire would bring their own spoon and small bowl to share the pudding. While this pudding party might suggest a similarly inspired recipe in the next few pages, we've reserved pudding for a few other feasts and planned a more sophisticated homage to St. John's Eve with a sweet summer wine and a shrimp and lobster dish you can share with friends around the bonfire.

Summer Wine for around the Bonfire

Also known as a Potus Ypocras. Ypocras was a very popular medieval beverage, and many different directions for preparation still exist. Also called Hippocras, the drink is named after the famous Greek physician Hippocrates.

Ingredients

1 bottle Riesling, or another mildly sweet
   white wine
1 cup honey
¾ cup elderflower liqueur
8 whole cloves
2 apples, cored and cubed
1 cup seedless grapes
1 bottle prosecco

Directions

- Bring the wine and honey to a boil. Skim the scum (or bubbles) off the top as is boils. This process is called clarifying the honey. Remove from heat and let cool. In a pitcher, add the wine and honey mixture, followed by the remaining ingredients. Let the mixture sit overnight in the refrigerator.

- In a champagne glass, pour the prosecco halfway and add the summer wine, leaving room for you to spoon in some of that deliciously drunk fruit into the champagne glass. Be careful to avoid the cloves, as you don't want to eat/drink those.

Shrimp & Lobster in Vinegar

Goes a little too nicely with the summer wine!

Ingredients

1 large shallot, finely diced
½ cup water
2 Tbsp white wine vinegar
1 tsp coriander
1 Tbsp lemon juice
1 stick unsalted butter, cut into pats
¼ lb cooked lobster meat (we used tail meat)
½ lb cooked shrimp
¼ cup finely chopped fresh parsley
2 cloves garlic, finely diced
Shavings from Parmesan Romano

Tip: Use a vegetable peeler to get nice, long shavings of cheese. It looks pretty fantastic. You can make this as a dinner serving or as an appetizer; either is delicious. We served this as an appetizer, along with grilled roasted garlic bread. It was meant for four, but the two of us devoured it in no time.

Directions

❧ In a saucepan, on medium heat, add the shallot, water, vinegar, coriander, and lemon juice. Stir. Allow it to reduce by a half. This is something you will need to watch—too little liquid will make it too thick, while too much liquid will make it runny.

❧ Using a whisk, add one pat of butter and stir. As it starts to melt, add another. Keep doing this until all the butter is gone and you have been continuously whisking. Remove from heat. Add the lobster and shrimp to the mixture and blend.

❧ Put the pan back on the heat and cook until the seafood is warm, just a few minutes, giving it a stir ever so often to prevent sticking or burning. Pour the seafood mixture into a nice, fancy deep dish or a pretty bowl. Add the parsley, followed by Parmesan shavings to the top.

St. Swithin's Day

July 15th
If it rains on this day, your next forty days are going to be very, very soggy.

The History
Rain or Shine?
According to legend, when St. Swithin was just a mere bishop, he asked to be buried outside where the rain could fall upon him. For nine years, his body did in fact remain outdoors (buried, of course), but the monks of Winchester decided to move his remains to a shrine, believing he was too great to be buried in such a humble location.

On that day, July 15, 971, heavy and horrible rains ensued, which led to the tale that if it rains on this day, it will rain for the next forty days! A gorgeous and sunny St. Swithin's Day, on the other hand, meant forty days of glorious weather. This tale predates the twelfth century and was passed along through the years.

It is said that Henry VIII wanted to put an end to all the myths surrounding St. Swithin, so much so that he had the shrine at Winchester destroyed

Rainy days and martyrs always get me down
Swithin was born in the year 800, somewhere near Hampshire, England. He died of natural causes in 862. He is the patron saint of Hampshire, Winchester, Southwark, and, of course, the weather.

(looted). This was a bit bizarre as it was also the location of his late brother's birth! Everything from the original shrine was demolished in the middle of the night so as to avoid public outcry. Pretty sneaky, Henry. A new shrine was built in 1962.

St. Swithin's day if thou dost rain
For forty days it will remain
St. Swithin's day if thou be fair
For forty days 'twill rain nae mair.

"Right as Rain" Apple Pastries

These are far too delicious to last forty days.

Apples desperately need rain at this point in the season. Without it the harvest would be scarce, and no one likes a bad apple. We recommend using McIntosh, but you can also use Granny Smith apples for a more tart dessert. Red Delicious is another variety that works well for this recipe.

- Always use cold tools with the pastry; this makes it much easier to cut the dough. We chill our cutters in the refrigerator for ten minutes before use.
- To make even sweeter pastries, sprinkle powdered sugar on top just before serving.

Ingredients

½ stick butter
1 apple, cored and cut into small cubes
1 Tbsp currants
2 tsp ground ginger
1 7-oz container almond paste
2½ tsp sugar
Salt, to taste
1 puff pastry sheet, thawed
1 egg, beaten
⅓ cup honey
⅓ cup mead
Vegetable or canola oil

Directions

⚜ Melt the butter in a medium size saucepan. Add the apple cubes, currants, and ginger to the pan. Once the apple is soft, remove the pan from the heat to allow cooling.

⚜ In a food processor, add the almond paste, breaking it up as you add it into the bowl. Next, add the apple mixture along with the sugar and a pinch of salt. Blend in the food processor. Your mix should resemble the texture of sand. Put the completed mixture in the refrigerator until you are ready to use.

⚜ Place the thawed pastry sheet onto a lightly floured surface. Roll out the dough until thin, but not so thin that you can see through it. Using a cutout or a biscuit cutter, cut out round circles in the pastry. Place a small scoop of the almond and apple mixture in the round, toward the bottom center.

⚜ Using a beaten egg, brush the outside circumference of the cutout round with the egg wash and fold. Using your hands, press the seals together firmly. This will give you a pastry shaped in a beautiful half-circle. Once you have completed the task, put the pastries on a cookie sheet and tuck them into the refrigerator to chill.

People of the Middle Ages also believed that if it did rain for forty days, this was the bishop's way of blessing the apple crops.

❧ While the pastries are chilling, add the honey and mead to a saucepan. Bring the mixture to a boil, skimming any foam off the top. Reduce the heat to medium low and let simmer to allow the sauce to thicken. If you are going to use immediately, remove the sauce from heat or try to keep it slightly warm in preparation for the next step.

❧ Preheat the oven to 375°F. Heat the oil on the stove top in a heavy pan until hot. Remove the pastries from the refrigerator and add them to the hot oil. Watch them carefully, ensuring that they do not burn, and turn them over when they are a light golden brown. When they are finished, place the browned pastries into the honey and mead mix, giving them a nice bath on both sides. Do this quickly. Finally, place the pastries on a lined cookie sheet (we use a silicone mat to keep them from sticking; you can also use parchment).

❧ Bake completed pastries in the oven for 25 minutes. They will puff up nicely.

Lammas Day

August 1st

Summary: Carb loading.

The History

Loafing Around

Lammas Day, or Loaf-Mass Day, is a festival celebrating the wheat harvest and was primarily celebrated in England and Scotland.

Predictably, it's all about the bread. Those who celebrated Lammas Day brought loaves of bread to church that were made from their new crops harvested at Lammastide (the season of, yup, bread). The loaves were blessed and then taken home to be broken into quarters and placed at all four corners of their property as a sign of protection for the crops.

It was customary for people in the villages to present freshly harvested wheat to their landlords, which was called "the feast of the first fruits." This tradition was referred to as the Gule of August and marked the end of the hay harvest. It was also customary to release a sheep into the fields—and whoever caught the sheep could keep it.

There are references to Lammas Day in Shakespeare's *Romeo and Juliet*: "Come Lammas Eve at night shall she be fourteen." The significance is that Juliet, turning fourteen before the harvest festival, did not live long to reap what she had sown.

The Greatest Thing Since Sliced Bread . . .

Medieval bread was similar to what we call whole-wheat bread. This was a staple in the everyday diet, so much so that it was rarely included in recipe books because everyone already knew how to make it. Trencher bread was what people used as disposable plates: a four-day old stale loaf was cut into thick slices and used as an eating surface. Peasants on the other hand missed out a bit; they used wood for their plates so as to not waste anything edible, and if wood wasn't available they ate directly off the table. Fresh trencher bread was used for elaborate (and expensive) feasts. Offering noble diners a "fresh cut trencher" with every course of the meal was considered good manners. Oddly enough, these nobles rarely ate the trencher.

Wheat, rye, and barley were the most popular grains used for breads; however, bad crops led the peasants to come up with creative alternatives, for example horse bread, which was made with beans and peas (not horses), and tourte bread, which contained corn husks.

We've developed our own trencher bread, and because this holiday falls in the hot month of August, we're suggesting a lovely salmon, cream cheese, and caper spread to go on top. However, you can also use this recipe for stews during the colder seasons, for example lamb stew (page 52). Yum.

Bread Winner

This "home plate" features a smoked salmon, lemon, and caper spread over herbed trencher bread.

Trencher bread is a dense bread with very little rise. This recipe stands up very well to fresh lemon juice, and the spread is so delicious and easy.

Ingredients for Trencher Bread

2 tsp sea salt or kosher
2 Tbsp lemon zest
3 fresh rosemary sprigs
1 tsp peppercorns
2 Tbsp sugar
1 cup warm water
2 tsp active yeast
3½ cups bread flour

Directions for Trencher Bread

⚜ With a mortar and pestle, combine the sea salt, lemon zest, rosemary needles, and peppercorns until they are combined. Set aside.

⚜ In a bowl, combine the sugar and water, followed by the yeast. Allow the mixture to sit for 10–15 minutes. You will know when it is ready when you see that the yeast has frothed and bubbled.

⚜ In a separate large bowl, add the flour. Slowly incorporate the yeast mixture into the dough, followed by the herb mixture. Using either your hands or a machine, knead the dough until all the ingredients are incorporated and the dough rolls neatly into a large ball. If it is too sticky, add a bit more flour; if it is too dry slowly add small amounts of warm water until you get the desired consistency.

⚜ Cut the ball in half. Using a rolling pin, flatten the dough to a somewhat longish piece. Remember: this dough will be used as a flat plate-like vessel for you to slice and serve with food later . . . and you also want it to look pretty! The traditional trencher bread had a lip around the sides and a "trench" going down the middle, but we are going to keep it simple and not do that here.

⚜ Grease a large baking pan and place the rolled dough onto the pan. Cover the dough with a damp cloth and store it on your counter until it doubles in size. This takes anywhere from 1½–2 hours, depending on the temperature of your home.

If you are fortunate enough to have a proofer setting in your oven, that would be the most ideal option.

❧ Once the dough is ready, heat the oven to 375°F and cook for approximately 20 minutes. The bread is done when it starts to develop a golden color.

Ingredients for Smoked Salmon, Lemon, and Caper Spread

8 oz mascarpone
2 tsp fresh dill
½ cup fresh lemon juice
2 Tbsp capers
2 cups arugula
4 oz smoked salmon
Salt and pepper, to taste

Directions for Smoked Salmon, Lemon, and Caper Spread

❧ Combine the mascarpone and dill in a bowl, and set aside.

❧ In a small bowl or jar, combine the lemon juice and capers.

❧ While one of the loaves is warm (tuck the other loaf away for dinner), smear the mascarpone mixture over the top. Next, cover the mascarpone with a layer of arugula, followed by a layer of salmon.

❧ Cut the salmon-topped bread into individual appetizer portions and lay them on a serving dish. Pour the lemon and caper mix over the top of the salmon bites, and salt and pepper to taste. You may not need a lot of salt due to the capers.

Pig Face Day

September 14th

Celebrated in Avening, England. Live high on the hog and always say "I'm sorry" with a pig's head.

The History

Pay Your Penance in Pork

One would think a feast named "Pig Face Day" was surely a spoof on someone who was not very good-looking, but that is not the case. This holiday is a nod to Queen Matilda, the wife of William the Conqueror, and is only celebrated in Avening, a quaint little village located in the Cotswold district of Gloucestershire, England.

In the eleventh century, Matilda fell madly in love with the handsome and manly Lord Brittric of Avening. He did not feel the same way (really?!). So, she did what any woman would do when faced with unrequited love . . . she threw him into a dungeon (what a power trip) where he remained until he died. Historians suspect that poison was involved in his untimely death.

Feeling incredibly guilty for her, um, well-known and very public temper tantrum, she commissioned a church in his hometown (how thoughtful). The church was consecrated in 1080, and the lovely

The Church of the Holy Cross in Avening, England, has been active and operating since it was consecrated in 1080. Parishioners still honor ancient traditions, including the Pig Face Day Celebration.

Matilda gave the builders a pig's head to feast on when the job was complete. This is the only church in history to be commissioned by a queen of England.

The feast still goes on to this day. Villagers attend a religious ceremony at the church and then dine on all things pork throughout the town. There's music, a hog roast, a torchlight procession, drinking, etc., all in the name of the teeny-tiny jealous queen, Matilda.

Matilda of Flanders became Queen of England in 1066 (officially crowned on May 11, 1068) and had nine children with William I. Two of those children went on to become kings, William II and Henry I. There are some documents that claim she was the tiniest Queen to ever reign at a mere four-foot-two, but there are conflicting reports in the research. Regardless, the little Matilda packed a powerful punch. During her coronation, the archbishop of York was instructed to speak to the importance of her role, and he declared that she was divinely placed there by God, that she should have share in royal power, and that she blessed her people by her power and virtue. Wow, heavy.

Wee Matilda's Big Pig Out

Fried pork balls with sage crème.

Meatball Ingredients

2 cups uncooked ground pork
1 egg, beaten
7 Tbsp panko
½ tsp allspice
¼ tsp ginger
¼ tsp pepper
Pinch cloves
Pinch ground saffron
1¼ salt
4 fresh sage leaves, finely cut; plus a dozen sage
  leaves, whole

Tempura Batter Ingredients

1 cup flour
1 Tbsp cornstarch
½ cup seltzer water
Salt to taste
Lard (you can use canola oil)

Sage Crème Ingredients

2 Tbsp butter
1 large shallot, minced
2 Tbsp minced fresh sage
¾ cup mead
¾ cup heavy whipping cream

> This is a perfect appetizer for any time of
> the year. Garnish the serving plate with fresh
> sage; its scent smells better than any candle's.

Meatball and Tempura Batter Directions

❧ Mix all the meatball ingredients and the four sage leaves in a large bowl. Mold the mixture into circles to form meatballs. Parboil the meatballs for 10 minutes. Place meatballs on paper towel to cool.

❧ While the meatballs are boiling, mix together flour, cornstarch, seltzer, and salt to taste. Mix until smooth. Let sit for 10 minutes.

❧ Melt a hunk of lard in a heavy pan. After the lard has heated up over medium to medium-high heat, take two forks and toss the cooled meatballs into the tempura batter.

❧ Turn the meatballs gently in the lard until the tempura is golden. It doesn't have to look perfect . . . as long as it tastes good. Once the meatballs are finished, toss the whole sage leaves in the tempura batter (about a dozen) and give them a quick fry in the hot lard. Garnish the meatballs with the crème and a piece of crispy sage.

Sage Crème Directions

❧ Melt 2 tablespoons of butter in a heavy pan. Toss in minced shallot and minced sage. Once the shallot is soft, pour in the mead and stir. Pour in the whipping cream and stir. Boil down by half until thick, on medium high.

The Installation of Archbishop Neville's Feast

September 1465

Showcase your immense wealth and power . . . then maybe don't get arrested.

The History

Living High on the Hog

Held at Cawood Castle near York, this feast lasted for many days and involved an unfathomable amount of food. There was no doubt that the appointment of George Neville as archbishop of York called for something spectacular. With 6,000 guests in attendance, the inventory of food served was quite extensive. George Nevill was richer than God and sought to prove it. The feast was a display of all his earthly riches and heavenly power.

George Neville (1432–1476) was the Archbishop of York and Chancellor of England. He was the youngest son of Richard Neville, 5th Earl of Salisbury, and Alice Neville, 5th Countess of Salisbury. His brother, Richard Neville, the 16th Earl of Warwick, was well-known throughout the land and was nicknamed "The Kingmaker." Reading all these stuffy titles makes us hungry, though perhaps not for peacock, swan, or porpoise.

95

Richard III (then the duke of Gloucester) was one of the many in attendance. George's nieces were also present: Isabel, who later married the duke of Clarence, and Anne, who went on to marry Richard III. This proved to be the beginning of George's downfall in later years—he presided over the weddings of both of his nieces, which caused him to fall into disfavor with the House of York. At the Battle of Barnett (a big moment in the Wars of the Roses), the earl of Warwick, George's brother Richard Neville, was killed, and George was taken prisoner. He was eventually released, shortly before he died in 1476.

Clearly, money isn't everything.

The following is a list of the food consumed at the feast:

From *De Nova Villa: or The House of Nevill in Sunshine and Shade* by Henry J. Swallow, 1885

Wheat: 300 quarters

Ale: 300 tuns

Wines: 100 tuns

Ipocrass (cordial wine flavored with spices):
  1 pipe (a "pipe" = a half ton)

Oxen: 104

Wild bulls: 6

Muttons: 1,000

Veals: 304

Porkes: 304

Swanns: 400

Kidds: 204

Cranes: 204

Chickens: 2,000

Pigeons: 2,000

Connies: 4,000

Heronshaws (young heron): 400

Pheasants: 200

Partridges: 500

Woodcocks: 400

Curliews (large bird from sandpiper family): 100

Egrits: 1,000

Cappons: 1,000

Geese: 2,000

Piggs: 2,000

Plovers: 400

Quailes: 1,200

Rees (female sandpipers): 2,400

Peacocks: 104

Mallards and teals: 1,000

Staggs, bucks, and roes: 500

Cold pastries of venison: 4,000

Parted dishes of jellies: 1,000

Plain dishes of jellies: 3,000

Cold baked tarts: 4,000

Baked cold custards: 3,000

Hot pastries of venison: 1,500

Hot custards: 2,000

Pikes and breams: 308

Porpoises and seals: 12

Spices, sugared delicates, and wafers: Plenty

"Swimming against the Tide" Salmon Pie with Parsnip Mash

Neville's conflicted loyalty lying in pastry.

Ingredients

Poaching liquid (this is what we used, but this is where you can customize according to taste)
   3 cups water
   2 cups mead
   1 carrot, sliced
   1 celery, sliced
   2–3 pieces fresh sage
   ½ medium onion, quartered
   1 lemon, sliced
1½ lb skinless salmon filets
4 leeks
4 Tbsp butter, unsalted
2 cloves garlic, finely chopped
2 eggs
1 cup, plus 4 tablespoons, heavy cream
2 tsp salt, plus more for taste
1 tsp pepper, plus more for taste
1 tsp coriander
2 tsp lemon zest
2 lb parsnips, peeled and sliced into 1-inch pieces
2 rounds Sandland Savory Piecrust (if you are using our recipe on page 18; if not your recipe should include enough dough for a deep-dish pie)

Directions

- ⚜ Poaching:

  - In a medium saucepan, add water, mead, carrot, celery, sage, onion, and lemon. Boil on medium-high heat.

  - While waiting for the mixture to boil, generously season salmon with salt and pepper.

  - Once the mixture hits a boiling point, gently lay the salmon filets into the water. Lower the heat to medium. Depending on the thickness, the salmon should be cooked in 5–8 minutes.

  - Remove the salmon and place into a bowl. Once slightly cooled, flake the salmon with a fork. Discard remaining mixture.

- ⚜ Rinse and trim leeks, removing root ends and dark green leaves. Slice the remaining vegetable into ½-inch rings. Soak the leeks in a bowl of cold water for 10–15 minutes and then drain. Set aside.

- ⚜ Melt 2 tablespoons of butter in a sauté pan, on medium heat. Add the cloves of garlic and fry until fragrant. Add the drained leeks and sauté until soft. Remove from heat and cool.

- ⚜ In a large bowl, add flaked salmon, 1 egg, 1 cup of heavy cream, 1 teaspoon of salt, pepper, coriander, and lemon zest. Mix, then add the cooled garlic and leeks. Gently incorporate.

- ⚜ Heat the oven to 350°F. Fill a large pan with salted water and bring to a boil. Add parsnips, and lower heat to medium and simmer.

- While the parsnips are cooking, prepare the savory pastry dough. Flatten each piece, separately, out onto a flour surface until the dough is slightly larger than a deep-dish pan. Line the deep-dish pan with a single round of dough. Pour the salmon mixture over the dough in the deep dish.

- Once the parsnips are soft, remove from heat and drain. Add the parsnips to your food processor, along with 1 teaspoon of salt, 4 tablespoons of heavy cream, and 2 tablespoons of butter.

- Whip until the vegetables resemble mashed potatoes. Add the parsnip mash to the top of the salmon mixture. Finish the pie by adding the second dough round to the top.

- The dough should overlap the pan a bit. Cut away the excess while pinching the top dough layer to the bottom dough layer. Finish the pie by brushing the top with the remaining egg (whisked).

- Cook for approximately 30 minutes, or until the top is golden.

Kingmaker's Chicken

A savory pie fit for a king, or, uh, archbishop. Or both.

Ingredients

1½ lb chicken thighs
4 pieces fresh sage
Olive oil
2 cloves garlic, minced
1 fennel bulb; peeled, sliced, cored, and with
  greens removed
1 large onion, diced
7 eggs
1 tsp ground ginger
1 tsp salt
1 tsp pepper
9-inch piecrust (Sandland Savory Piecrust on
  page 18 is preferred, but you can use store-
  bought piecrust)

Directions

⚜ Partially poach the chicken in water with 2 whole pieces of sage. Once chicken is partially cooked, remove from the stove top, let cool, and chop into bite-size pieces. Set aside.

⚜ In a sauté pan, heat a coating of olive oil. Add the garlic first and fry until fragrant, followed by the fennel and onion. Once soft, remove the vegetables and set aside.

⚜ Preheat the oven at 400°F. In a large mixing bowl, add the eggs and whisk. Add the cooled chicken and vegetables (if your chicken is too hot it will cook the eggs too quickly). Next, add the ginger, salt, and pepper. Fully incorporate and pour the mixture into the pie shell.

⚜ Bake in the oven for 45 minutes.

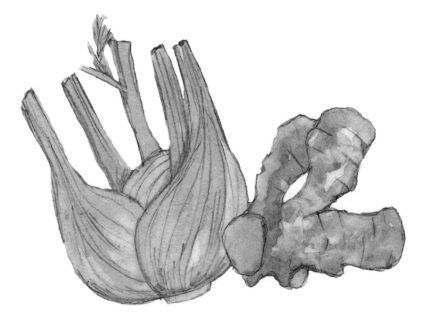

Michaelmas

September 29th

Feast of St. Michael, the Archangel. Get goosed.

The History

The Goose Is Getting Fat . . .

This day marked the end of the harvest, when rent and debts were due. It is one of the four quarter days, all of which meant you had to pay up: Lady Day (March 25), Midsummer (June 24), Michaelmas (September 29), and Christmas (December 25). Days were shorter, and the hunt for winter meats began.

Michaelmas was often referred to as "Goose Day." There are two possible reasons for this: First, when Queen Elizabeth I was told that the Spanish Armada had been defeated (July 29, 1588), she ordered everyone to eat goose on Michaelmas, mainly because that's what she was eating when the news arrived; second, rents and debts were often paid in food and often in the form of a goose. Eating goose on this day meant good luck and prosperity for the new farming cycle.

St. Michael the Archangel is the patron saint of the sea, ships, boatmen, horses, policemen, and horsemen. He is singlehandedly responsible for defeating Lucifer and casting him down from heaven. Michael is the leader of the everlasting battle against evil, and he guides departed souls to the next world. He watched over Adam and Eve after they were kicked out of Eden, and even taught Adam how to farm. Busy guy.

Eat a goose on Michaelmas Day, Want not for money all the year.

Eating all sorts of birds was customary for the times. Geese were popular for their feathers as well as their fat. Most were hunted by nobility as a sport, but, as mentioned, the lower-class also used them as payment of debts.

Other birds popular on the medieval plate were partridge, pheasant, quail, ducks, chicken, capons, peacocks, doves, puffins, swan, cranes, and heron. The swan was really only consumed by royalty, and, to this day, one must get permission from the queen if they'd like to cook one.

Duck, Duck, GOOSE!

The ancient Egyptians ate goose, but its popularity was at its height in the Middle Ages. Most Americans are not familiar with the cooking and eating of a goose. It can be quite tricky (and a little intimidating), but fear not! We shall walk you through the process.

Here are some tips that will help you "get goosed." First off, you can use duck or turkey instead with our recipe. Cooking times may vary. If you are, in fact, up for the goose challenge, note that geese consist of all dark meat and have a very intense flavor. Be brave, be bold. Talk to your butcher.

For this recipe, we recommend using a fresh, young goose that weighs 8–10 pounds (closer to 10; geese breasts are not as meaty as a duck, turkey, or chicken). The good news is that geese are not mass produced in the states and are mostly hormone-free. Your bird should be fatty—but white-fat, not yellow-fat (ick).

Keep the fat. Goose fat is ideal for adding amazing flavor to french fries or, uh, anything else. It can be a very decadent substitute for butter. These birds are very greasy, so it's important to syphon the fat and keep lots of towels on hand. Be sure to read our hints throughout the recipe, and just go for it. No risk, no reward.

Give Them the Bird

Roasted goose with honey glaze and figs. You will need a turkey baster and fat separator.

Ingredients

Whole goose, 8–10 pounds, giblets removed
2 cups very hot water
½ cup honey
3 sprigs fresh sage
3 sprigs fresh thyme
2 tsp salt
2 tsp pepper
1 tsp dried sage
1 tsp cardamom seeds
2 apples, cored and chopped
6 carrots, chopped
¼ cup chicken stock
2 Tbsp butter, cubed
4 figs, quartered

Ingredients for Gravy

2 Tbsp butter
2 Tbsp flour

> **Get your fig on.** Did you know that a fig, usually considered a fruit, is actually an inverted flower? Seek out the smaller figs that have a delicious, sweet smell.

Directions

⚜ **Prepping your goose**: Like you would when shopping for a duck, look for a plump goose. If not, you will end up with a perfect amount of delicious cooking fat but not a lot of meat to serve your guests. Goose is not easy to find, so ask your grocery store butcher if they are able to order one for you. They are usually happy to assist you. If your goose was previously frozen, it is best to thaw it out for more than 24 hours in your refrigerator. Once that has taken place, remove the bird from the refrigerator and let sit for at least 30 minutes, bringing it closer to room temperature.

⚜ Remove the giblets (do what you wish with them, but don't ask us; they make us a little squeamish). Cut the excess fat

Women also collected wild carrots the week before the Michaelmas feast. They used a three-pronged mattock to dig a triangular hole around the carrots in order to pull them from the ground. This hole represented St. Michael's shield and the three-pronged shovel represented his trident.

with kitchen shears, as well as the outer wings. We know that sounds strange but there is a *lot* of fat on these birds and the outer wings are virtually meatless. Rinse the bird thoroughly inside and out, then pat dry. Preheat the oven to 425°F. Place the bird breast side up on a racked pan.

❧ Using a fork, firmly prick the fat on the breast (try not to hit the meat) 15 to 20 times. Pour 2 cups of hot water over the bird and let it rest for 10 minutes, then pat dry. This tightens the skin to help you render the fat, resulting in a beautifully browned bird.

❧ In a saucepan, add the honey and clarify (remove the foam). Keep on the stove top slightly warmed. In the bird cavity, add the fresh sage and thyme. There is *not* a lot of room in there. Lightly tie the legs together with cooking twine. With a mortar and pestle, combine the salt, pepper, dried sage, and cardamom seeds. Grind the spices together to release the fragrances. Spread the rub over the breast of the bird and then flip the bird on the roasting pan until it is breast down.

❧ This is where we are going to caution you on the cooking process. Goose has a lot of fat and this will be evident when you put it in the oven. The oven rack should be placed in the middle (to accommodate the size but also to limit splattering). This is not the kind of poultry that you can put in the oven and run over to your neighbor's for a glass of wine while you wait. You have to be around to watch the goose, flip it as recommended, and to remove the fat as you go along. *You got this.*

❧ Using your turkey baster, remove the pools of hot fat that end up in your roasting pan with some frequency. Don't throw it out; instead, put it into the fat separator. This is going to be important for your gravy later on (and it is also fabulous with potatoes). Unless you have a very large roasting pan, you will need to take extra measures to contain the fat as the legs might extend beyond the pan. We placed our roasting pan on a baking sheet and wrapped the end of the legs in aluminum foil to prevent them from burning. You will also want to tuck the neck fat into the body (on the goose, that is).

- Brush the bird with the honey and place the roasting pan in the oven for 30 minutes, at 425°F. While this is cooking, place the apples, carrots, chicken stock, butter, and figs in a separate baking dish. Mix it together nicely and pop it into the same oven.

- After 30 minutes, remove the pan from the oven and flip the bird. *Don't do this in the oven.* Baste the breast with honey. We also dabbed our brush into the fat and mixed it with the honey on the bird. Put the bird back in for 30 minutes, breast side up. After these 30 minutes, remove the bird from the oven and baste using the honey/fat mix once again.

- Lower the oven to 350°F. Flip the bird again, breast side down. Remove the separate baking pan with the apples and carrots. Add these to the roasting pan, evenly spread around the bird. Pop back into the oven again for 30 minutes.

- Repeat the technique one last time, turning the bird breast side up and baste with honey. This time, remove the fat carefully from the pan using the baster and put into the fat separator. You will notice that the fat is really pooling up at this point and you will need to keep a good eye on everything.

- Cook the bird for another 30–60 minutes breast side up, until the internal temperature of the thickest part of the legs reaches 175–180°F. And, yes, it will look pinkish; you heard us right. Once done, remove from the oven and let it rest for at least 20 minutes.

- Remove the bird from the rack and place on a cutting board. Remove the vegetables and fruit and place in a bowl. Pour any remaining fat into the fat separator. For this recipe, you want to keep the fluid that is a darker, richer color, not the fat. Pour this dark, rich fluid into a bowl, reserving the remaining fat in a container and put in the refrigerator. You can use this at a later time for recipes that require fat.

- To make the gravy, melt 2 tablespoons of butter and add 2 tablespoons of flour in a saucepan. When it starts to brown, pour in the richly colored fluid to flavor the gravy. Stir and cook on medium heat until it begins to thicken.

- Slice the goose meat, arrange the vegetables and fruit on a plate, and serve with the delicious gravy.

I dig what you're digging. In Scotland, there is a very specific food associated with this day—Saint Michael's bannock, also known as Struan Michael. This bread-cake is made from various grains harvested from one's land. These grains were mixed with sheep's milk and sweetened with fresh honey.

Saintly Fall Fritters

Parsley, sage, rosemary, and thyme . . . and tarragon . . . and beer.

Ingredients

1 Tbsp yeast
½ cup lukewarm water
2 cups all-purpose flour
1 tsp salt
Preferably fresh and finely chopped:
    1 cup flat leaf parsley
    1 Tbsp tarragon
    2 Tbsp rosemary
    2 Tbsp sage
    1½ Tbsp thyme
Lard
1 cup Summer Shandy (if you cannot find a
    summer citrus beer, look for a pale ale and
    add lemon)

Directions

❦ Dissolve the yeast in the water, and set aside until it bubbles up.

❦ In a separate bowl, combine the flour and salt, then add the herbs, Summer Shandy, and mix. Pour the yeast water into the mixture and combine thoroughly. It should be a thick, smooth consistency. Cover and store in a warm place until the mixture has doubled in size.

❦ Heat the lard in a deep, heavy pan until it is hot. We know; lard often gets a bad rap, but good lard is made from natural ingredients, has been used for centuries (so it's not going to kill you), and has the ability to cook cleanly at a high level. Our favorite part about using lard is the gentle flavor it imparts to the food, and it leaves a less "oily" feel to fried foods. You get the point.

❦ Drop a spoonful of the batter into the lard. We would recommend doing a test fritter to check the temperature and mixture. Once you get going, we recommend adding a few at a time. The fritters will puff up a bit and become golden—that is your sign to remove them from the liquid.

❦ Using a slotted spoon, move the fritters to paper towel–lined plates. If you need a little something extra, add some salt if you like your food salty, or add honey if you want it a little sweeter.

> The Michaelmas Daisy (aster) blooms during the fall, when all other flowers seem to be fading. They are said to bloom for St. Michael as a tribute for conquering evil, standing out against the gloom of decay.

September 29th Blackberry Butter and Lemon Scones

Be sure to make this on September 29th; you don't want to mess with the devil.

Ingredients for Blackberry Butter

1 lb softened, unsalted butter
6 oz blackberries
½ cup honey
½ tsp cinnamon
¼ tsp salt

Ingredients for Lemon Scones

These are proper English scones, which are smaller and generally round—perfect for afternoon tea.

2 cups all-purpose flour
2 Tbsp sugar
½ tsp salt
1 Tbsp baking powder
½ cup plus 1 Tbsp buttermilk
2 tsp lemon zest
1 egg, beaten
⅓ cup butter

Directions for Blackberry Butter

* In a standing mixer, add the butter and beat until it is light.

* Add the remaining ingredients and mix the blackberries slightly. You want the butter to change to a beautiful light purple, but you want to prevent the blackberries from being completely mashed.

* The butter mixture fits beautifully into three jam jars. Eat one and give away the other two as gifts.

Directions for Lemon Scones

* Heat the oven to 400°F. The butter is the most important part of the process. Without proper handling, your scones will not be flaky. Freeze the butter until it is solid and ready to use.

* In a large bowl, add the flour, sugar, salt, and baking powder and blend. In another bowl, mix the buttermilk, lemon zest, and egg.

* Remove the butter from the freezer and use a cold cheese grater to cut the butter into the flour. The less you touch the butter, the better. With a wooden spoon, gently combine the butter and flour. Make a well in the center of the flour and pour in the buttermilk mixture.

* Mix the ingredients together for just a minute. Place the dough on a well-floured surface and use your hands to form a ball. Gently flatten the ball and, using a rolling pin, roll out the dough to about an inch thickness.

* To get that wonderful flaky layer in the center of the scone, fold the dough over once and then gently roll it out again to an inch thickness. Using a biscuit cutter, cut out round layers of dough and place it on cookie sheet that is covered with a silicone mat or parchment paper.

With the extra dough left, repeat the process and roll the dough out again and cut a round, as described above, until all the dough is gone or is unusable. Pop the pan into the oven for 10 minutes, then turn the pan and cook for another 6–8 minutes. Once the scones are done, remove from the oven and spread lemon glaze over the top. Serve with blackberry butter and clotted cream, of course.

Ingredients for Lemon Glaze

2 tsp lemon zest
¼ cup powdered sugar
1 Tbsp lemon juice

Directions for Lemon Glaze

Mix all ingredients together until smooth.

As mentioned, there seem to be specific superstitions associated with most of the medieval holidays. For Michaelmas, one should not pick blackberries on September 30. What? People during the medieval times believed that when the devil was struck from heaven, he landed on a blackberry bush and cursed the fruit forever. Supposedly, he renews this curse every year on Michaelmas Day. So, go ahead and make this jam the day before. You never know!

All Hallow's Eve

October 31st
Summary: Get me my broom!

The History

As one might guess, All Hallow's Eve was what we now know as Halloween. October 31, the night before All Saints' Day, was a time of spiritual unrest. A deep fear of the dead drove the villagers to burn fires and wear costumes to confuse any wandering spirits. Soul cakes were left on doorsteps to feed ghosts and were also brought to your neighbor's house so that they, too, could pray for the dead and their journey to other worlds. The line between this world and the next was especially fragile on this night, so all superstitions were attempts to prevent any crossovers.

What's with All the Other Halloween Stuff?

Most of the symbols we associate with Halloween date back to the Middle Ages. Witches, for example, were said to come into their power on this night. As a result, on All Hallow's Eve, many took to old superstitions in an attempt to protect their homes "from the effects of witches." These wicked women accompanied the wandering spirits who roamed free during the night. This thinking had evolved from a pagan holiday, Samhain, which celebrated "the crone" or "earth mother." All Hallow's Eve is in fact a Christian form of this pagan holiday. The crone was always described as having a cauldron, where souls were kept until their reincarnation. Creepy.

Black cats had always been considered to be bad luck as far back as the Dark Ages. Solitary women who happened to own black cats were labeled witches and their pets were called "familiars" (a demonic creature given to them by the devil that would do their bidding and commit horrible atrocities). Bats were also believed to be a witch's familiar. Seeing a bat fly around your house on Halloween indicated imminent death for one of its residents, and you would be haunted by evil spirits. We never liked bats anyway.

Spiders, too—if one fell into a lit candle, there were surely witches nearby. And in case you were wondering, candy corn was not associated with Halloween until the 1880s.

The Medieval Witch

Cunning folk, wise women, white witches, healers, midwives, seers   all of these were legitimate professions in the Middle Ages. These women were sought after for their healing remedies, cleaning solutions, herbal lotions, love spells, and medical advice, among other things; that is, until the hysteria that led to massive witch hunts began in the fifteenth century. In 1486, a book known as the *Malleus Maleficarum* (The Hammer of Witches) was written by Heinrich Kramer, a German Catholic clergyman. Although witch trials had already begun as early as the ninth century, this book seemed to put a giant spotlight on witchcraft as an evil curse on the world and as something that needed to be destroyed.

As with most witch hunts, times were tough and fraught with disease, poverty, war, drought, and religious or political turmoil. People were compelled to blame their misfortunes on someone or something. Although it was mostly women who burned at the stake for false crimes and bogus accusations, many men and children were prosecuted as well.

Squash Your Demons with Honey and Almonds

Witchy fall flavors to nibble on while you stir the cauldron.

Ingredients

1 butternut squash
½ cup honey
4 Tbsp unsalted butter, melted
⅓ cup sliced almonds
¼ tsp cinnamon
Salt and pepper, to taste
Thyme, to garnish

Directions

❧ Heat the oven to 400°F.

❧ Using a sharp knife, carefully cut off the bulb portion of the squash. The bulb portion is the only section that you are using for this recipe; save the rest for later cooking. Stand the bulb portion right side up and cut the squash, top to bottom, into four quarters. You will be left with four wedges of squash.

❧ Scoop the seeds from the squash and discard. Flip the squash over and slice a very small piece of the skin off so that the squash sits flat.

❧ In a bowl, combine the honey, melted butter, almonds, and cinnamon. Place the squash in an oven-safe bowl or pie plate, and pour the honey mixture over the top. Salt and pepper to taste.

❧ Cook the squash for 35–40 minutes until the squash is soft and golden. Garnish with thyme.

The Crone's Scone; a Deconstructed Pork Pie

Save your soul and eat some deconstructed pork pie.

Ingredients

1 sheet puff pastry, thawed
3 Tbsp butter
3 sprigs fresh thyme
1¼ tsp salt
1 tsp pepper
1⅛ tsp cinnamon
1 tsp ground ginger
½ tsp nutmeg
1½ lb pork loin cut, trimmed into 12 medallions
1 small onion
1 apple, diced
2 tsp finely minced gingerroot
¾ cup chicken stock
1 cup mead (or sweet white wine)

Directions

❧ Heat the oven to 350°F.

❧ Roll the puff pastry out on a floured surface until it achieves a ½-inch thickness. Using a biscuit cutter, make small rounds in the pastry and place them on a lined cookie sheet.

❧ Melt 1 tablespoon of butter in a pan and stir in one sprig of thyme. Use a pastry brush to apply the butter on the top of the pastry rounds. Place rounds in the oven and bake until golden.

❧ Meanwhile, in a shallow bowl combine 1 teaspoon each of salt, pepper, cinnamon, ground ginger, and nutmeg. Gently press each side of the pork loin into the mixture and set aside.

❧ In a sauté pan, melt 1 tablespoon of butter on medium heat. Sauté the onion and apple together until soft. Stir in the gingerroot and cook for a minute. Add the chicken stock, mead, and remaining salt and cinnamon. Cook on medium until the sauce is reduced by half.

❧ While the sauce is reducing, heat the remaining butter in another pan over medium to medium high heat. Working in batches, add the pork medallions and cook until medium rare. This only takes a minute or two on each side. The pork will cook quickly, so be careful not to overcook: using your finger, press into the pork as it cooks. If the pork is firm but not hard, there is a good chance that it is done.

❧ Remove the meat from the pan and add to the reduced sauce until thoroughly coated. Add the remaining thyme to the mixture and stir gently.

❧ Assemble the mixture on a plate with the pork medallions first, followed by a spoonful of the onion and apple, drizzle on some reduced sauce, and top it off with a puff pastry round. Salt and pepper to taste.

Martinmas

November 11th

Bundle up and get your meat ready. Winter is coming.

The History

Where's the Beef?

Martinmas, or St. Martin's Day, was when the wheat seeding was completed and the annual slaughter of fat cattle began in preparation for the winter. This beef was salted and preserved for the cold months ahead. So, while your beef is hanging in the barn, have some of our duck ravioli instead.

The Man with Many Hats

St. Martin (Martin le Miséricordieux) was born sometime in the fourth century. He was forced by his family to become a soldier with the Roman Army. One day, he saw a poor, cold man lying on the ground, and he cut his own cloak in half to cover the beggar. This is when Jesus appeared to him, and the divine encounter caused him to leave the army, get baptized, and devote the rest of his life to the needy and the poor. He is the patron saint of poverty, beggars, cavalry, equestrians, geese, hotel-keepers, innkeepers, wine growers, and wine makers. One could say St. Martin wears many hats.

Like Michaelmas, Martinmas was also a time for geese. Rumor has it that St. Martin once hid in a goose pen to avoid being ordained as bishop. Hence, a cooked goose was often part of the celebration. Goose was expensive, so duck was a common meal substitute for the peasant folk.

The phrase "your goose is cooked" may have come from the fourteenth century when a Czech priest named Jan Hus (1372–1415) was burned at the stake for being a heretic. His last name, Hus, sounded like "goose"; also, "husa" translates to goose. So, when he burned, one could say his goose was cooked. Another theory for the origin of this phrase is that it came from the sixteenth century. When Eric the Mad of Sweden raided a small town, the residents hung a goose outside their houses to show their enemies they were not starving. Angry at the defiance, Eric and his cronies set fire to the town, thus cooking the goose. What a waste.

This holiday originates from France, but it had already spread to most of Europe by the Middle Ages. In Ireland, it was custom to sacrifice a rooster and sprinkle some of his blood in the four corners of your home (messy). Families also believed it to be incredibly bad luck to let any sort of wheel turn on your land. This was because St. Martin had been tossed into a millstream, and he was killed by its wheel. Ouch.

Meanwhile, in Germany and the Netherlands, it was custom to have giant bonfires, which led to the nickname Funkentag or Spark Day. Youngsters would leap through the flames of these bonfires and spread ashes on fields to make them fertile.

Peasant Duck Ravioli

With shallots and pancetta.

Ingredients

1 whole Rohan duck from D'Artagnan, 5½–6
   pounds
2 cups boiling water
3 tsp anise seeds
24 juniper berries
½ tsp salt
¼ tsp pepper
1 Tbsp butter
2 cloves garlic, minced
2 shallots, minced
2 tsp fresh sage, finely chopped
8 oz mascarpone cheese
1 egg
Perfect Pasta recipe (pg 17)

Directions

❧ Preheat the oven at 425°F, with a rack in the center.

❧ Remove the duck from the wrapping, and trim the wingtips (they will burn if you don't). Remove any items in the body cavity. Thoroughly rinse the inside and outside of the duck with water.

❧ Place the duck, breast side up, on a roasting pan. We recommend using a deep roasting pan that comfortably fits the length of the duck. Using a fork, liberally prick the duck's skin. Be careful, as you want to go deep enough into the skin but not into the flesh. Pour the boiling water all over the skin that you have just prepared. This tightens the skin so that you will get a beautifully roasted bird. Allow the bird to cool for a half hour.

❧ While you wait, combine the anise, juniper berries, salt, and pepper in a mortar, and grind with a pestle until you get a nicely ground mixture. After the duck has cooled, pat the duck with paper towels, inside and out. Rub the entire bird with the mixture. Focus on the breast, but save some for the inside as well.

- Pop the duck in the oven for 45 minutes, breast side up. Remove the duck from the oven and carefully turn the duck over to breast side down for another 45 minutes. After that, once again remove the duck from the oven and turn it over, breast side up. You will also want to remove the fat from the pan using a baster or by simply tilting the pan. You can save this fat for future cooking, like with potatoes or eggs. Cook for a final 45 minutes.

- After 2¼ hours, the duck will be golden and simply delicious. Remove the duck from the oven and let it rest. After it has cooled, you will be able to shred around 5 cups of meat.

- Melt butter in a sauté pan, over medium heat. Add garlic, followed by shallots, and stir for 2 minutes. Add the sage, and stir and cook for another minute. Remove from the stove.

- In a large bowl, combine the duck meat, cooled shallot mixture, mascarpone, and egg until fully incorporated.

- Roll out the pasta dough on a floured surface and make ravioli the way you choose; either by hand with a cutter template or with a machine. Fill the ravioli with the meat mixture. As long as you are sealing the dough together properly, it will hold. Use a spray bottle to lightly spray the edges of the pieces of dough with water, and use a pastry brush to make sure it is covered completely.

- Store the raviolis in the freezer on a cookie sheet lined with flour until frozen. You can use them right away or place them in a plastic bag for future use.

Cinnamon Beef Roast Wrapped in Heaven

Go heavy on the wine; we won't say anything.

Ingredients

3 lb roast
2 tsp each cinnamon, salt, black pepper
1 tsp ground ginger
½ tsp each cloves and nutmeg
½ lb pancetta, sliced
Olive oil
2 cloves garlic (we used ½ clove elephant garlic)
2 medium onions, sliced
2 medium carrots, diced
2 ribs celery, diced
½ lb mushrooms (we used baby bella), sliced
1 Tbsp rosemary, fresh
3 stems thyme, fresh
2 bay leaves
3 cups burgundy wine
2 cups beef stock
½ stick unsalted butter
4 Tbsp all-purpose flour

Directions

⚜ Pat the beef dry with a paper towel. In a large mixing bowl, add the cinnamon, salt, pepper, ginger, cloves, and nutmeg. Mix until fully blended. Add the beef into the bowl and rub the mix into all sides thoroughly. You will have some mix left over; set aside for later.

⚜ Allow the meat to sit for approximately 20 minutes or until it reaches room temperature. Wrap the beef in pancetta on all sides. If you are feeling fancy, you can truss the meat. YouTube has great videos on how to truss. If you can't get the trussing down, make multiple ties around the beef with kitchen string, since the meat needs to be evenly cooked for the best results. If your roast is at different thicknesses, it will have parts that are overcooked or undercooked.

⚜ In a Dutch oven (or large oven-proof pan), heat a nice coating of olive oil on medium heat. At this point, we added some of the remaining spice mix to the pancetta-covered beef, pressing it nicely into the pork. Just so you know, this part smokes like the dickens—prepare yourself. Crisp all sides of the beef in the olive oil, and then remove roast and set aside.

⚜ Preheat the oven to 325°F. In the Dutch oven, over medium heat (still on the stove top), add the garlic. We really like to use elephant garlic. Technically this is not garlic but fennel, though it has a mild garlicky taste. It also slices like heaven. Once the garlic starts to brown, add the onions until they begin to soften.

⚜ Add the carrots and celery until they start to soften. Toss in the mushrooms followed by the fresh rosemary, thyme, and bay leaves. Stir and then add the burgundy and beef stock. Stir again. Gently place the roast into the Dutch oven, cover, and roast in the oven for 90 minutes.

Added bonus: We decided to deconstruct this meal the next day. We cut up the meat and heated it with the remaining sauce, serving it over pasta. To make it especially fabulous. we heated up some bacon fat (butter will also do) and tossed some panko crumbs in the hot liquid until toasty. Finally, we sprinkled the toasted panko over the pasta to give an extra crunch to the leftovers. So good.

- Remove the pan from the oven and carefully take out the roast, placing it aside. Cover loosely with aluminum foil.

- Place the *very* hot Dutch oven onto the stove top, over medium heat. Cook down the juices for 20 minutes. Remove the bay leaves.

- It is now time to make a roux. In a separate pan, heat ½ stick of butter until melted over medium to medium low heat. As the butter begins to bubble, sprinkle the flour into the butter and stir, stir, stir. Remove a cup of juices from the Dutch oven and slowly mix it into the roux. Remove from heat and pour the roux into the Dutch oven, then stir. Sprinkle with fresh thyme.

- Cut the meat and serve with the gravy.

The original version of this recipe dates back to fourteenth century France.

Last of the Harvest Chutney

To serve with Peasant Duck Ravioli (you can replace chutney with pea puree on page 64).

Ingredients for Harvest Chutney

½ cup honey
1 apple, cored and diced
1 pear, cored and diced
2 cups pitted and chopped cherries (we used sweet red cherries that are not sweetened; if they are not in season, most freezer sections have frozen unsweetened cherries that are delicious)
¼ cup packed brown sugar
½ cup white wine or champagne vinegar
½ cup currants
1 tsp ground ginger
⅛ tsp ground cloves
¼ tsp cinnamon
¼ tsp white pepper

Directions for Harvest Chutney

- In a heavy pan, heat the honey. Once the honey is hot (but not boiling), remove the white skim off the top.

- Stir in apple, pear, cherries, brown sugar, white wine or vinegar, currants, ground ginger, cloves, cinnamon, and white pepper.

- Cook for 20–25 minutes. Once the mixture gets thick, remove from the stove top and store, or use right away on the fabulous ravioli you just made.

St. Martin's Sickness Prevention

Hair of the dog, hangover remedy—whatever you want to call it, it will make you feel better.

Martinmas was definitely a joyous holiday. No somber religious observances, just lots of food and beer. Those who had a little too much drink were called "Martinmen." One should also note that, along with his long list of patronage responsibilities mentioned previously, St. Martin was also the patron saint of tavern keepers and drunkards. So much mead, ale, and wine were consumed that the hangover that followed was dubbed "St. Martin's sickness."

Since this breakfast is meant for those "delicate" mornings, you may want to make the batter a day in advance and store it in the refrigerator. The best part of this breakfast is that you can eat the items separately or put them all together to make a sandwich. We recommend that breakfast be served with our version of a mimosa—a half glass of champagne, with the other half filled with equal parts St. Germaine and orange juice.

Ingredients for Waffles

1 lb regular cut bacon
2 cups all-purpose flour
1½ tsp baking powder
2 Tbsp sugar
1 tsp salt
¼ tsp pepper
2 large eggs
1⅔ cups buttermilk
⅓ cup heavy cream
⅓ cup butter, melted
1 cup shredded cheddar cheese
¼ cup parsley

Directions for Waffles

❧ Slice the bacon into bite-size pieces. Cook the bacon in a heavy pan until crisp but not burned. Remove the cooked bacon and place on a paper towel; set aside.

❧ In a large mixing bowl, combine the flour, baking powder, sugar, salt, and pepper.

❧ In another bowl, combine the eggs, buttermilk, and heavy cream. Whisk slightly. Carefully pour the ⅓ cup of cooled melted butter into the wet mixture and combine. Slowly pour the wet mixture into the dry mixture, mixing constantly with a wooden spoon. The mixture should be free of lumps.

❧ Add the cheddar cheese, bacon, and parsley to the final mixture to complete the batter.

❧ Heat some butter in a pan and make your waffles.

To make waffle sandwiches, we used a waffle pan instead of a waffle iron to make smaller, uniform waffles.

Ingredients for Waffle Sandwiches

4 Tbsp butter
1 large onion, sliced thin
1 Tbsp sugar
1 Tbsp cinnamon
1 Tbsp ground ginger
2 Tbsp brown sugar
1 tsp ground cloves
½ tsp white pepper
1 lb center-cut bacon
Cold large eggs
1 capful white vinegar
A creamy sauce of your choice; our favorite is a
   simple blender-style Béarnaise sauce

Directions for Waffle Sandwiches

- **To make caramelized onions:** Heat 2 tablespoons of butter in a sauté pan on medium heat. Once the butter is melted, add the onion and then sprinkle with sugar. Cook the onions until they are golden brown, stirring occasionally to prevent sticking. Once done, remove from heat and set aside.

- **Candied bacon:** Combine the cinnamon, ginger, brown sugar, cloves, and white pepper in a shallow bowl. Press the bacon into the mixture, coating both sides. Add the bacon to a hot pan. As the bacon candies, it may burn if unattended, so watch it carefully. If you notice the bacon starting to smoke, add a tablespoon or two of butter to the pan to prevent burning. The bacon will become gloriously sticky. Once done, also set aside.

- **Poached eggs:** Do *not* be intimidated by poached eggs. They are shockingly easy and you do not need any fancy tools. Simply heat a medium-size saucepan. Add salted water and heat to a rolling boil. Add a capful of white vinegar and lower the heat to medium low, letting the water settle down to a simmer. Crack an egg into a cup first. Get the cup close to the water and gently slide the egg into the hot bath. Cook for about 4 minutes. You can add a few more eggs to the bath but it may take a half minute or so longer to cook. Remove the eggs with a slotted spoon and add on top of the sandwich.

- To make this wonderful sandwich, start with one waffle. Add the caramelized onion and a slice (or two) of candied bacon, followed by the poached egg and a dollop of Béarnaise sauce. Top with another piece of waffle to complete the sandwich.

- We made this for brunch. It was the quietest brunch we ever had, as our friends could not stop eating these "day after" treats.

St. Andrew's Day

November 30th
Celebrate Scotland, pray naked.

The History

X Marks the Spot

St. Andrew is the patron saint of Scotland (also of Russia, fishermen, singers, unmarried women, and would-be mothers). He became their patron saint sometime in the tenth century and was believed to have been a fisherman. Unfortunately for him, Andrew was crucified on a tilted cross, or an "X"-shaped cross, because he did not feel worthy of being put up on the same cross as Jesus. This tilted cross has been on the Scottish flag for over a thousand years.

St. Andrew's Day traditions have transformed over the years—where it was once a religious observance, it has now come to be a celebration of Scottish culture. In the village of St. Andrews, this holiday is a week-long festival of music, games, plays, and traditional Scottish fare. Now we're talking!

Sweet Dreams

Like many other medieval holidays, there are several superstitions associated with the day. Young women would say the St. Andrew's prayer while naked, then would kick a straw bed, in order to have visions of a potential husband. Um, okay. In Romania, girls would put grains of wheat under their pillow before falling asleep so that they would dream about their potential husbands.

This seems a lot more reasonable than naked bed-kicking.

That's *Not* Beef

One of the most notable dishes that hails from Scotland is haggis. Most of us cringe when it's mentioned, but this dish has taken on a more modern flavor profile. Chefs in Scotland have found delicious ways to serve up this savory pudding of minced meats, onions, and spices. Yes, it's all thrown into an animal's stomach and stewed, but we can get over that, especially when it is served with a creamy mustard sauce! (Scottish folk are most probably cringing if they read this; most of them are purists when it comes to haggis.)

We chose to skip over the haggis (leave that to the pros) and tackle an old Scottish recipe—Atholl Brose.

Atholl Brose Whip on Tipsy Oatcakes

Go home, cookie, you're drunk.

Ingredients for Atholl Brose

2 cups Drambuie
½ cup rolled "old fashioned" oats
¼ cup honey
2 cups heavy cream
½ tsp nutmeg, plus some extra for garnish
2 Tbsp confectioners' sugar

Ingredients for Drunken Oatcakes

1 stick unsalted butter, softened
⅓ cup sugar
1 egg
Oatmeal from Atholl Brose
¾ cups all-purpose flour
½ tsp salt
⅛ tsp cinnamon

Directions for Atholl Brose (a three-day process)

- Mix the Drambuie and oatmeal together in a container with a lid. Store the liquid in a cool, dark place for two days.

- At the end of the second day, strain the oatmeal from the liquid; however, do not throw the oatmeal away. That is a key ingredient to make for our drunken oatcakes. Add the honey and store the liquid in the refrigerator for another day.

- On the third day, add heavy cream in a stand mixer, and whip. As the mixture is forming stiff peaks, add the nutmeg and confectioners' sugar. By now, the liquid should be thick and ready to use.

- Pour the liquid from the refrigerator into a large bowl. Gently fold the whipped cream into the liquid and repeat until the liquid is incorporated into the whipped cream. If you have "over folded" the cream and it seems flat, you can add it back to the mixing bowl and whip. It will not get back to what it once was, but it will help quite a bit.

- Once the dessert is ready, you can serve it in a glass bowl along with the drunken oatcakes and a generous sprinkle of nutmeg.

Directions for Drunken Oatcakes

- Preheat the oven to 325°F. In a mixing bowl, cream together the butter and sugar until light and fluffy. Scrape the bottom of the mixing bowl to ensure that all the butter is mixed with the sugar.

- Add the egg and mix into the butter. Once fully mixed, add the drunken oats, flour, salt, and cinnamon.

- Generously grease an 8x8-inch cake pan and press the batter into the pan. Cook in the oven for 25 minutes until the oatcakes

are soft but firm to the touch. Immediately use a small cutter to cut out the oatcakes and put onto a cookie rack.

✤ Sprinkle with nutmeg or cinnamon. Do not throw out the remaining crumbles from the pan. Put those in a container and use as garnish for the Atholl Brose . . . or just gobble them up; we won't tell.

Atholl Brose gets its name from the 1st Earl of Atholl, John Stewart. Stewart was a Scottish nobleman and ambassador to England. In 1475, he filled a well with a concoction of oatmeal brose, honey, and whiskey so that the Highland rebels would get tipsy and be easily captured. Very sinister, but very delicious. As the recipe developed, cream was added later on, and we're not complaining.

Zut Alors!

⚜ Food in medieval Scotland consisted of all sorts of meats: mutton, beef, and veal as well as wild birds such as swans, geese, pheasants, and peacocks. The meats were expensive, so the products produced by their game and cattle (innards, dairy, and eggs) were more commonly used for sustenance.

⚜ In Scotland, everything was sweetened with honey. Their vegetable selection was limited to things like cabbage, leeks, and onions. Wheat was difficult to grow in the damp climate, so their main source of carbohydrates was oats.

⚜ Mary Queen of Scots should be thanked for introducing French cuisine to the country. When she returned to Scotland in 1561, she brought back a full staff of French chefs that changed Scottish flavor profiles forever. *Mon dieu!* The combination of two cultures resulted in some unique cooking terms: cannel (cinnamon), gigot (a leg of mutton), and howtowdie (a boiling fowl), just to name a few.

⚜ French cuisine in medieval times consisted of a wide variety of meats, roasts, and rich sauces as well as complicated desserts, delicate pastries, and sugared fruits.

Pies of Paris

A French dish for a Scottish queen.

Ingredients

1½ lb pork roast, cubed into 1-inch pieces
1½ lb beef roast, cubed into 1-inch pieces
Flour
Olive oil
4 oz diced pancetta
1¼ cup red wine
1 cup chicken broth
1½ cup currants
1 cup diced dates
8 egg yolks
1½ tsp salt
1 Tbsp ginger
2 Tbsp sugar
9-inch pie shell
1 sheet of puff pastry
1 egg, set aside

Directions

❧ Preheat oven to 375°F. Take the pork and beef cubes and lightly roll them in flour, shaking off any extra flour. Swirl olive oil in the bottom of the pan to coat. Add pancetta to the pan until it starts to crisp. Now add the beef, then the pork, to the pan. Sauté for just a few minutes, until the meat is warmed but not cooked thoroughly. Remove all of the meat from the pan.

❧ Deglaze the pan to get all those great crispy bits up: add the red wine and chicken broth to the pan. The remaining traces of flour will add a thickness to the liquid as it starts to boil. Once at a boil, add the meat back into the pan. Lower the heat and simmer on low for 5 minutes.

❧ Remove meat once again from the pan, while reserving the cooking liquid. Place the drained meat in a large mixing bowl and cool for a few minutes. Add currants, dates, egg yolks, salt, ginger, and sugar into the bowl with the meat and mix together. Add ¼ cup of the cooking liquid into the mixture and mix thoroughly.

❧ Place the mixture into the 9-inch prepared pie shell. The mixture will be higher than the shell; our recommendation is to make a mound in the middle that slopes downward as you move out toward the crust. You can add more liquid, but the more you add the runnier it will be (if that is your thing, go for it). Roll out the chilled puff pastry sheet and place it over the pie. Press the puff pastry and piecrust together, creating a seal, and cut away any excess puff pastry that hangs over the side. Whisk the remaining egg in a bowl and, using a pastry brush, lightly brush the egg over the puff pastry.

❧ Place the pie pan onto a cookie sheet (or some other pan that can catch juices if they were to bubble over; this is especially important for all you people who like it extra runny). Put into the oven and cook for 45 minutes. Remove from the oven (it should be a lovely golden color on the top), and set aside to cool for no less than 10 minutes. Cut into slices and serve warm.

Christmas

December 25th
Whassup wassail? Easy on the drink, this is a serious holiday.

The History

Christmas during the medieval times was far different from Christmas today. The church made sure it was a solemn event focused on the birth of Christ. The word itself first appears in the eleventh century as "Christes Maesse," meaning "festival of Christ." The church tried to ban any form of merriment at this time, but it didn't really work out. Gifts were still exchanged, dancing and singing ensued, and there was more food than you can possibly imagine.

Presentation Is Everything!
Giant, elaborate feasts were the main theme. Every meal was labored over with careful consideration of presentation. Swans were plucked and cooked, only to have their feathers placed back on the cooked dish so it appeared live. The poor bird was then decorated with gold, marzipan, and pastry. Clearly a health hazard, but pretty (in a creepy way).

Not-Your-Auntie's Mince Pie
Some traditions did carry over, for example, mince pie. The medieval mince pie was a tiny bit different than the fruit-based mince pie your aunt brings over for Christmas dinner. This one had meat in it. Yup, real meat. Turkey was not served during this time, but the meal always included fowl, venison, or beef along with a boar's head, and possibly a peacock or (gilded) swan. Wassail and wine flowed, and puddings were abundant.

Food during Christmas was incredibly important and decorative for both nobles and peasants. Crops were harvested by this point in the year and animals that would not make it through the winter were slaughtered for the table. Supplies were fairly abundant as Christmas occurred just before the harsh winter months really kicked in. The poor were not expected to work and were often given food gifts from nobles such as geese. In 1482, King Edward IV hosted an enormous Christmas feast and fed nearly 2,000 of his people. Although these banquets were considered to be generous and kind, they were most likely a power play and an exhibition of wealth.

Christmas carols do originate from this time period, but they were banned for a short time because this meant singing and dancing in a circle, which disrupted the religious ceremonies. Trees were decorated with apples on Christmas Eve, but they were placed outside instead of in the living room, as Christmas trees are today. Plays were a common form of entertainment, nativity statues were built, and holly and ivy were used for decorations. Santa Claus was not part of any traditions, but St. Nicholas did have a popular feast day on December 6.

Short Rib Lasagne

We wish you a merry Meatmas. This is our version of a meat pie.

PASTA PLEASE! You can, of course, buy your lasagne. If you go that direction, see if your grocery store stocks fresh flat sheets of pasta. Store bought, hard lasagne is okay if you have no choice, but it is *way* more impressive to make your own. If you are feeling ambitious and want to go for it, refer to our pasta recipe on page 17.

Ingredients for Short Ribs

1 cup plus 2 Tbsp flour
Salt
Pepper
4 lb short ribs (find the meatiest ones you can; go to the butcher counter rather than grabbing one from the meat section).
Olive oil
1 Tbsp butter
2 carrots, sliced
2 stalks celery, sliced
2 garlic cloves, minced
1 large onion, chopped
2½ cups burgundy wine
2½ cups beef stock
5 sprigs thyme
2 sprigs rosemary
1 sprig tarragon
1 cup chopped fresh flat-leaf parsley

Directions for Short Ribs

❧ Preheat oven to 325°F. Mix 1 cup flour, salt, and pepper in a bowl. Be generous with the salt and pepper as it helps with the flavor of the meat. Dredge the ribs in the flour mixture and coat on all sides. Drizzle enough olive oil in a Dutch oven to coat the bottom of the pan, turn the flame to medium heat, and wait until it is nice and hot.

❧ Working in batches, cook ribs until browned on all sides, about 6–8 minutes per batch. Remove the ribs and put them aside until later.

❧ Add the butter to the Dutch oven. Add carrots, celery, minced garlic, and onion and cook until softened, stirring often, about 10 minutes. Sprinkle the remaining 2 tablespoons of flour over the vegetables. Stir for about one minute and the flour will begin to brown at the bottom of the pot.

❧ Add ½ cup of the burgundy wine and stir for about 1 minute until almost all liquid is absorbed, scraping all those tasty browned bits from the bottom of the pan. Add remaining red wine. Bring to a boil, then simmer until reduced by about ⅓, stirring often, about 7 minutes. Add beef stock, thyme, rosemary, tarragon, and 1½ teaspoon of salt and 2 teaspoons of black pepper.

- ✤ Return to boil. Return ribs to pot, arranging meat side down in single layer. Cover pot and place in oven to braise ribs until very tender, about 2¼ to 2½ hours.

- ✤ Remove the pan from the oven. Using tongs, take the ribs from the Dutch oven and place them in a separate plate, allowing them to cool. Once cooled, *using your hands*, shred the beef and discard the bones. While shredding, remove the tough connective tissue and excess fat, as no one will enjoy eating that. You will be left with a mound of beautifully shredded beef. You will notice that there is a layer of fat on top of the cooled mixture in the Dutch oven. Spoon that off and discard responsibly (i.e., not down your sink).

- ✤ Boil sauce until reduced to 5½ cups, about 8 minutes. Return meat to sauce. Season sauce to taste with salt and pepper. Stir in chopped parsley. Shut stove off and let the mixture cool.

Ingredients for Béchamel:

5 Tbsp unsalted butter
¼ cup all-purpose flour
3 cups whole milk
½ tsp nutmeg
½ tsp salt
¼ tsp pepper

2 cups pecorino grated cheese

Directions for Béchamel

- ✤ Melt butter in heavy, large saucepan over medium heat. Add flour and whisk until smooth. Cook until light golden brown, whisking frequently, about 6 minutes.

- ✤ Add milk and bring to boil, whisking constantly, about 1 minute. Add nutmeg, salt, and pepper. Cool slightly.

Assembling Your Lasagne

- ✤ Preheat oven to 375°F. Butter the baking dish, paying attention to the bottom especially.

- ✤ Place your first layer of lasagne sheets in the dish and spread 1 cup of the delicious meat sauce over, followed by a layer of about 2–3 tablespoons of grated pecorino cheese.

- ✤ Lay another layer of sheets down, but this time spread 1 cup of béchamel over the pasta evenly. Sprinkle pecorino again.

- ✤ Repeat layers until you get to the final, top layer. Brush melted unsalted butter over the top layer, followed by a heavy sprinkle of pecorino.

- ✤ Bake the lasagne uncovered until the edges are bubbling and the top is golden brown in spots, about 45 minutes. Let rest for 10 minutes.

Loaf around the Veal Pie

Perfect for company, or if you want something to eat while you hide from company.

Ingredients

1 carrot, peeled and sliced
1 leek, trimmed
2 cloves garlic
Olive oil
2 lb ground veal
2 cups baby spinach, finely chopped
2 tsp salt
⅓ tsp allspice
1 tsp black pepper
6 large eggs
2 rounds Sandland Savory Piecrust recipe
   (page 18)
1 cup plain bread crumbs or panko

Directions

❧ In a food processor, chop the carrot, leek, and garlic. Process until finely chopped. This should only take a few moments.

❧ Heat olive oil in a large sauté pan, over medium heat. Add the vegetables from the food processer to the hot pan, watching carefully to ensure they do not brown or burn. Once the vegetables are soft, add the veal.

❧ Using a wooden spoon, break down the veal to make sure there are no large pieces and the veal browns evenly. Cook for 10 minutes and add the chopped spinach.

❧ As the veal is cooking, hard-boil 3 eggs in a separate saucepan. Once the eggs are done, remove from water, cool, and peel. Before you remove the veal, add the remaining salt, allspice, and pepper, and mix together. Remove from heat and set aside to cool. Set the oven to 400°F.

❧ Roll out the two dough rounds, separately, on a floured surface. You will be using a loaf pan for this meal, so the dough should be rolled out to fit this type of pan. Grease the pan with butter and line the inside of the pan with the first piece of dough. The greatest thing about the Sandland Savory Piecrust recipe, if you are using it, is that the dough is forgiving. If you make a tear, you can pinch it back together.

❧ In a large bowl, add the veal mixture followed by 2 whisked eggs and the bread crumbs. Mix all ingredients and add it to the dough-lined loaf pan. Using your hands, make 3 wells, equal distances apart, for the hard-boiled eggs.

❧ Add the whole eggs and cover with veal mixture. Cover the mixture with the remaining dough piece. Keep in mind that the top will eventually become the bottom after the cooking process. We cut the dough to perfectly fit the top of the pan and then used the remaining dough from the bottom to overlap and seal with an egg wash.

⚜ Bake for 30 minutes, or until golden. Remove from the oven and cool slightly. Invert a serving plate over the top of the pan, and, in one swift move, flip the pan and the serving plate. Remove the pan very gently.

"Christmas Is Coming" Pork Rolls

With creamy coriander dipping sauce.

Ingredients

2 large cloves garlic, finely diced
1-inch piece of fresh gingerroot, finely diced
2 Tbsp olive oil
1 large shallot, finely diced
1 lb ground pork
1 tsp black pepper
1 tsp sea salt
1 tsp cinnamon
½ tsp cumin
1 egg, separated
1 package of egg roll wrappers
1 cup currants
Cooking oil (we used a mix of vegetable oil and
    bacon fat)

Ingredients for Coriander Dipping Sauce

8 oz crème fraîche
1½ Tbsp honey
1 Tbsp olive oil
1½ Tbsp ground coriander

Directions

❧ Sauté the garlic and ginger in the olive oil. Once fragrant, add the shallot. Be careful—these are three items that burn quickly, especially if they are diced finely. Once ready, add the pork and partially cook. (We are partially cooking the meat because the final cooking process will finish the job.)

❧ Remove from the pan and add to a mixing bowl. Cool for a few minutes and then add the pepper, salt, cinnamon, cumin, and egg yolk. Combine.

❧ Spread out an egg roll wrapper. It should look like diamond in front of you, rather than a square. Whip the egg white in a bowl. Brush the egg roll wrapper with the egg white on all sides. At the bottom of the wrapper, plop a tablespoon of the mixture. Fold the bottom corner and roll the mixture, tucking the sides in as you roll up. It will look a bit like a round envelope when you are done.

❧ These can be made in advance and tucked away in the refrigerator, but please cover with plastic wrap so they do not dry out.

❧ In a deep, heavy pan, heat the cooking oil until hot. To test the oil, either drop a bit of water in the oil or take a dry wooden spoon and dip it in the oil. If the oil bubbles for either technique, it is ready.

❧ Gently place a few of the completed rolls into the hot oil. We recommend medium heat; this prevents the items from burning and hopefully saves you from getting hit by a grease dart. Ouch. Once the rolls are brown on all sides, remove and place on a plate covered with a paper towel. Repeat the process for the remaining rolls. Note to self: don't eat right away or you will lose a layer off of your tongue.

❧ The dipping sauce is a breeze. Mix all the ingredients and combine fully. Dip away.

Crispels

Fried dough with honey is way better than dancing sugar plums.

> Crispels are simple pastries that are coated in honey. The original recipe dates back to the fourteenth century!

Ingredients

1 sheet puff pastry dough, chilled
½ cup honey
½ tsp cinnamon
1 Tbsp unsalted butter
Powdered sugar

Directions

⚜ Remove the puff pastry dough from the freezer and allow it to thaw a bit. While you are waiting for the dough to thaw, heat the honey and remove any foam. Add the cinnamon and stir, stir, stir. Keep warm.

⚜ Using a rolling pin, roll out the sheet of thawed puff pastry dough on a lightly floured counter. We used a chilled biscuit cutter, but you can use a round cookie cutter or trace an upside down teacup with a knife. Whatever you use, chill it first. *You're welcome.*

⚜ Melt the butter in a frying pan. Gently place the adorable little rounds into the butter. Fry the rounds on medium heat until brown and slight puffy. Add more butter as needed to keep the batches from sticking or burning. Remove the fried rounds and place on a paper towel.

⚜ Brush the pastries with the honey mixture and add a dash of powdered sugar. Eat warm. Yummmm.

About the Authors

Tricia Cohen grew up in a house with two kitchens surrounded by family, food, and love. In her adult life, she continues to share her love for food with the community as a gourmet home cook and sous chef. She lives in North Truro, Massachusetts.

Lisa Graves is the author and illustrator of the *Women in History* series. She recently illustrated *The Tudor Tutor* (Skyhorse Publishing) and is the creator of Historywitch.com, a site dedicated to illustrations and biographies of history's most fascinating characters. She lives in Medway, Massachusetts.

You can keep up with their journey into food history on the Facebook page Deconstructing History One Bite at a Time.

Index